URBAN
TRAILS
SALT LAKE CITY

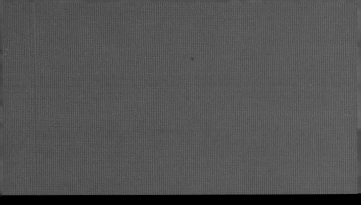

URBAN
TRAILS
SALT LAKE CITY

**Salt Lake Valley · Trans-City Routes
Millcreek · Cottonwoods**

ASHLEY LAUREN BROWN

**MOUNTAINEERS
BOOKS**

MOUNTAINEERS BOOKS is dedicated to the exploration, preservation, and enjoyment of outdoor and wilderness areas.

1001 SW Klickitat Way, Suite 201, Seattle, WA 98134
800-553-4453, www.mountaineersbooks.org

Printed in China
Distributed in the United Kingdom by Cordee, www.cordee.co.uk
First edition, 2023

Copyeditor: Emily Estes
Design: Jen Grable
Layout: Laura Shaw Design, Inc.
Cartographer: Ben Pease
All photographs by the author unless credited otherwise
Cover photograph: *Paintbrush lining the Brighton Lakes Loop (Hike 32)*
Frontispiece: *Sundial Peak catches the afternoon light at Lake Blanche (Hike 29)*

Library of Congress Cataloging-in-Publication Data is available at https://lccn.loc.gov/2023004054.
The e-book record is available at https://lccn.loc.gov/2023004055.

Printed on FSC-certified paper

ISBN (paperback): 978-1-68051-548-0
ISBN (ebook): 978-1-68051-549-7

An independent nonprofit publisher since 1960

CONTENTS

TRANS-CITY TRAILS

SALT LAKE CITY

MILL CREEK CANYON

MURRAY, MILLCREEK, AND HOLLADAY

COTTONWOOD HEIGHTS AND SANDY

BIG COTTONWOOD CANYON

LITTLE COTTONWOOD CANYON

DRAPER

WEST JORDAN TO HERRIMAN

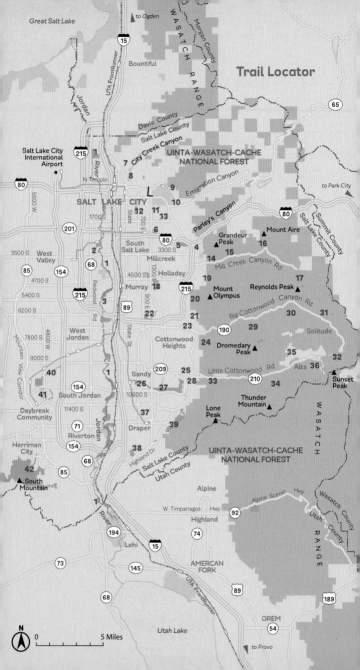

TRAILS AT A GLANCE

Trail/Park	Distance	Walk	Hike	Run	Kids	Dogs
TRANS-CITY TRAILS						
1. Jordan River Parkway	Up to 35 miles one way	•		•	•	•
2. Redwood Nature Area and Decker Lake	4.5 miles	•		•	•	•
3. Germania Park and Little Confluence	3-mile loop	•	•	•		•
4. Parley's Trail	6.2 miles one way	•		•	•	•
5. Parley's Historic Nature Park	2.4 miles	•	•	•	•	•
6. Sugar House Park	1.8-mile loop	•		•	•	•
SALT LAKE CITY						
7. Ensign Peak and Nature Park	4-mile loop		•			•
8. Memory Grove Park and City Creek Canyon	9.5-mile loop	•	•	•	•	•
9. Red Butte Garden	3-mile loop	•	•	•	•	
10. Governors Groves	1-mile loop	•		•	•	•
11. Miller Bird Refuge and Bonneville Glen	1-mile loop	•		•	•	•
12. Liberty Park	1.5-mile loop	•		•	•	•
13. Wasatch Hollow Preserve	1-mile loop	•	•	•	•	•

Trail/Park	Distance	Walk	Hike	Run	Kids	Dogs
MILL CREEK CANYON						
14. Pipeline Trail	9 miles one way		•	•	•	•
15. Grandeur Peak	6 miles		•	•		•
16. Mount Aire	3.8 miles		•			•
17. Dog Lake	6 miles		•	•	•	•
MURRAY, MILLCREEK, AND HOLLADAY						
18. Big Cottonwood Regional Park	4-mile loop	•		•	•	•
19. Neffs Canyon	5.5 miles		•			•
20. Mount Olympus	7 miles		•			•
21. Heughs Canyon	3.1 miles		•		•	•
22. Murray Canal and Wheeler Historic Farm	4.2 miles	•		•	•	•
COTTONWOOD HEIGHTS AND SANDY						
23. Big Cottonwood Canyon Trail	4 miles	•		•	•	•
24. Ferguson Canyon	4 miles		•			•
25. Quail Hollow	3 miles	•	•	•	•	•
26. Dimple Dell West	3.9 miles	•	•	•	•	•
27. Dimple Dell East	6-mile loop	•	•	•	•	•
28. Bells Canyon	4.9 miles		•			
BIG COTTONWOOD CANYON						
29. Lake Blanche	6.2 miles		•			
30. Donut Falls	3.6 miles		•	•	•	
31. Willow Lake Heights	2.6-mile loop		•	•	•	
32. Brighton Lakes Loop	4.5-mile loop	•	•	•	•	

Trail/Park	Distance	Walk	Hike	Run	Kids	Dogs
LITTLE COTTONWOOD CANYON						
33. Little Cottonwood Creek Trail	3.3 or 6.3 miles	•	•	•	•	
34. White Pine Lake	10.5 miles		•		•	
35. Cardiff Pass Trail	3.5 miles		•			
36. Albion Basin to Cecret Lake	5 miles		•	•	•	
DRAPER						
37. Mehraban Wetlands Park	1.1-mile loop	•		•	•	•
38. Porter Rockwell Trail and Draper Canal	7.2-mile loop	•		•	•	•
39. Bear Canyon Suspension Bridge	4.4-mile loop		•	•	•	•
WEST JORDAN TO HERRIMAN						
40. Bingham Creek Trail	3.2 miles	•		•	•	•
41. Oquirrh Lake Loop	3.2-mile loop	•		•	•	•
42. Blackridge	3.5-mile loop	•	•	•	•	•

INTRODUCTION

TRAILS FOR FUN AND FITNESS
IN YOUR BIG BACKYARD

"No, wilderness is not a luxury but a necessity of
the human spirit, and as vital to our lives as water
and good bread."

—EDWARD ABBEY

WHEN I BECOME DEPLETED and exhausted from endless
technological demands and the stress of living in a civilization
obsessed with speed, time and time again I find the cure in
nature. With my soles on the dirt, surrounded by the sights and
sounds of nature's true chaotic perfection, wild places nurture
and restore my weary soul. For me, a walk outside is often all it
takes to calm frazzled nerves and pixelated perspectives.

Urban Trails: Salt Lake City is a tool for exploring wild
places within the urban sprawl. My belief is that time spent
outside will heal, soothe, and invigorate our community. I
hope you delight in getting to know Salt Lake City's nature
sanctuaries, unbelievable geographical variety, and endless
adventure opportunities.

Opposite: *Autumn foliage along the Red Butte Garden trail (Hike 9)*

The truth about Utah's undeniable beauty is out. In fact, Utah ranks as one of the fastest-growing states in the nation. Population-growth experts estimate that within forty years, the population will increase by 2.2 million people. Salt Lake County, which includes Salt Lake City, the state capital of Utah, is the most populated area and is bursting with gems for nature lovers. The trails in this book explore the jagged Wasatch Peaks that rise suddenly and majestically from the valley floor and the globally esteemed canyons that snake up the mountains from the city proper.

While writing exclusively about exploring mountain peaks and canyons surrounding the city is tempting, that wouldn't do Salt Lake justice. The city and suburbs lie within the now dry lakebed of what was once the ancient Lake Bonneville. Countless streams drain from the mountains and foothills to the Jordan River, which flows south to north, spanning Salt Lake County. Wherever the water flows free, rich riparian (marshes and wetlands surrounding the watercourse) habitats cultivate thriving biodiversity.

A patchwork of protected acres, preserved land, creeks, and conservation easements make exploring the wilderness amid urban hustle possible. The walks and hikes featured in *Urban Trails: Salt Lake City* focus on areas where the natural habitat flourishes. While some of the routes are paved pedestrian paths, and several areas are essential city parks, there is one constant—the experiences outside will refresh and restore.

Over time, nature reveals a core truth: humans are not separate from the natural world. We are of it. When polarity and extreme perspectives dampen our lives, a wander outdoors melts barriers and brings out the best in humanity. Gentle smiles, polite nods, and laughing children remind us that we are more alike than not. This book aims to demonstrate how outdoor spaces are healing for humankind.

Throughout writing *Urban Trails: Salt Lake City*, my conviction remained steadfast—all people should be able to get

A walker passes by a blooming fruit tree in spring in City Creek Canyon (Hike 8).

out into nature. Here you'll find the directions, maps, and other data you need to experience the magic of mountainous rambles and neighborhood sanctuaries. It's a human right to spend time in wild places, and wilderness immersion is the first critical step in teaching our species how to be stewards.

This guidebook is a love song to humans, our fellow creatures, and Mother Nature.

This book features hikes in Mount Olympus, Twin Peaks, and Lone Peak Wildernesses.

HOW TO USE
THIS GUIDE

THIS EASY-TO-USE GUIDE provides you with the tools you need to curate a list of go-to spaces for moving freely outside and, in turn, falling in love with nature. The details are designed to empower each user, with the goal of encouraging folks from all walks of life to head out on the trails. The forty-two routes featured only begin to scratch the surface of Salt Lake's extensive network of mountain trails, riparian habitats, preserves, and green spaces. So explore the trails in this book, and don't stop there!

I have hiked, walked, or meandered every route (most of them many times) described in this book. I consulted multiple resources to ensure sound information. Trails, conditions, and parks can change, however, so it's wise to check on an area's status before embarking on an adventure.

THE ROUTES

In this book you'll find routes scattered throughout Salt Lake County, ranging from valley-floor explorations to high mountain peaks. Every route begins with an information block detailing the following:

Distance. This is the total length of the hike in miles. Unless otherwise noted, all distances are round trip. Mileage for every route was measured with a GPS tracking device, and the data was cross-referenced against information from land management groups and maps. However, the information in this guide might vary from other resources or personal data.

Elevation Gain. For most routes, this number represents the cumulative elevation gain for the entire trip, as measured by a GPS tracking device. The purpose is to provide an idea of the total amount of climbing involved, not an exact figure.

High Point. This is the highest point of elevation on a given route.

Difficulty. The difficulty rating is based on route length, elevation gain, and trail surface. Hikes in this book range from easy to challenging, with a fair representation of hikes in each category. Many of the trails in the valley of Salt Lake are easy or moderate, but the treks in surrounding canyons are often more challenging due to the steep grade and uneven surface of mountainous trails. Depending on personal fitness, you may find the trail easier or more challenging than described.

Time. This is the estimated length of time it will take to complete an entire hike. Depending on personal fitness, it may take more or less time than listed.

Fitness. This suggests whether the trail is suitable for walkers, hikers, or runners. Paved paths appeal to walkers and runners, while steep mountain trails are typically best for hikers. If the trail moves through natural vegetation, with a mellow grade and even surface, all three fitness levels are included. Don't let the designations deter you. Walk, hike, or jog at your own discretion.

Family-friendly. Here you'll find notes about ADA accessibility and whether strollers are suitable for the trail, as well as any other special considerations or areas for children. Most hikes are listed as family-friendly because children understand that walking outside is the destination. Parents will know how much vigor is appropriate for their child and when to turn around.

Jordan River Parkway's paved trail is perfect for wheelchairs, strollers and bicycles (Hike 1).

Dog-friendly. Find all information related to dogs in this section, including leash requirements and pup-related amenities like poop bags and waste receptacles. It's a dog owner's responsibility to clean up after their pet. So don't bring your pooch if you won't pick up their poop.

Amenities. These can include restrooms, parking, drinking water, picnic areas, interpretive signs, information centers, campgrounds, playgrounds, and more.

Contact/Map. This notes the agencies or organizations that manage the area. The website and phone numbers are listed in Resources. Many agencies provide downloadable or printed maps.

MAP LEGEND

[15]	Interstate Highway	▲	Summit
[89]	US Highway	▪	Building/Landmark
(154)	State Highway	⥵	Bridge/Boarwalk
[19]	Forest Road	⊶	Gate
	Surface Road	～	River/Stream
	Unpaved Road		Lake
----------	Hiking Route	⚘	Wetland/Marsh
- - - - - -	Go Farther Route	⫘	Falls
- - - - - -	Other Trail		Park/Open Space
$	Start		Other Park/Golf Course
P	Parking		National Forest/Wilderness
⚇	Restrooms/Privy		Campus
⚘	Picnic Area		Other Land
🏠	Picnic Pavilion	⊶☐⊶	UTA FrontRunner & station
⚑	Campground	⊶○⊶	UTA TRAX light rail & station
⚇	View/Overlook	⊪⊪⊪⊪	Stairs

GPS. GPS coordinates are provided for the main trailhead of each hike. Coordinates are based on the WGS84 datum.

Before You Go. Look here for park hours, fees, and trail popularity. Also noted are seasonal considerations like the best months for wildflowers, winter travel restrictions, and availability of shade. Also find information about wildlife, equestrian trails, and bike use.

GETTING THERE. Every hike includes a description of how to arrive at the trailhead. **Public Transit:** If the trailhead is accessible via Utah Transit Authority (UTA) public transportation, the best approach is listed here. When a route is serviced by bus and TRAX, typically the directions are from the TRAX station. I included as many trails with public transportation access as possible because most of the hikes in surrounding canyons require a vehicle. **Bike Route:** If the

A walker and leashed dog stroll around the pond at Liberty Park (Hike 12).

trailhead is accessible via bike, that information is noted here.
Driving: The directions are from the closest major city, highway, or interstate exit. Parking information and details about
seasonal road closures are also included.

EACH ROUTE begins with an overview designed to paint a
picture of the area by describing the geography, history, and
what to expect.

GET MOVING. This section includes step-by-step directions
that complement the route's map and aim at making navigation
a breeze. Views, places to rest, alternative turnaround points,
flora descriptions, and historical sites are also listed here.

GO FARTHER/GO FURTHER. Look here for ideas on how to
increase the outing length, get involved with local conservation organizations, or choose alternate objectives.

A NOTE ABOUT RESTROOMS

"Restrooms" in a national forest are usually simple vault toilets that are typically available for use year-round. Restrooms found around city and county parks and conservation areas range from well-maintained facilities with flush toilets and handwashing stations to standard chemical outhouses. Unfortunately, many park restrooms close during fall and winter (with the chance of freezing pipes), and the water is turned on again sometime in the spring. Sometimes chemical toilets are available when flush facilities are closed, but not always. This book mentions whether a trailhead has a restroom available, but we can't guarantee they will always be in service or in good condition.

GETTING TO KNOW SALT LAKE CITY

Understanding a bit about Salt Lake City's geography, weather, and climate makes for a more enjoyable experience. When you're informed about regional nuances, exploring is less stressful and also empowering!

GEOGRAPHY

Part of what makes Salt Lake an esteemed adventure hub is its unique geography. The city sits in a basin surrounded by mountains. The foothills of the Wasatch Range kiss the valley floor, and their sheer spires rise abruptly to the east. The Oquirrh Mountains climb to the west. Near the divide between Salt Lake and Utah County, the two ranges pinch toward each other in an area called "The Point of the Mountain." And then there's the city's namesake, the Great Salt Lake, which is a salty remnant from the massive, ancient Lake Bonneville, which existed 13,000 to 30,000 years ago.

Salt Lake City proper sits at 4300 feet above sea level as mountain peaks soar thousands of feet above the valley, many reaching heights over 11,000 feet above sea level. The high mountains capture moisture from passing storms and create an oasis. Deep, glacially carved canyons and snowmelt-

Thick smog hovers over Salt Lake valley during winter high pressure.

fed streams drain into the Jordan River and produce rich riparian habitats.

Salt Lake's majestic crown of mountain peaks also contributes to its infamously poor air quality. As the population booms—and while fossil fuels continue to be a primary energy source—the air quality worsens, especially with cold temperatures. Greenhouse gases get caught in the Salt Lake Valley by temperature inversion, and the thick fog of visibly toxic air hovers over the city, sometimes for weeks. During long periods of high pressure, Salt Lake's air quality ranks among the worst in the world.

Fortunately, the solution is (hypothetically) easy. During February and March of 2020, when the world slowed down with the onset of the global pandemic, Salt Lake's air quality took a dramatic turn. With the large drop in traffic volume, the air became healthy to breathe, even during periods of high pressure.

This lived experience demonstrates how crucial conscious commuting is for healthy air. That's why *Urban Trails: Salt Lake City* focuses on routes accessible via public transportation whenever possible. Choosing public transit is an individual choice that contributes to the health of the whole.

SALT LAKE CITY'S WATERSHED

A watershed is an area of land that collects, stores, and releases water into a single stream. The snow-fed streams that cascade down the glacially carved canyons of the Wasatch Mountains provide Salt Lake City with up to 60 percent of its drinking water. Fresh, clean snow melts into streams that reach residents' taps within 12 to 24 hours.

A few decades after the arrival of pioneers, the mountain streams and tributaries that feed the Jordan River and Great Salt Lake became so polluted they were dangerous to drink. Culprits included urban development, agricultural run-off, deforestation, and mining. In response, President

Theodore Roosevelt in 1904 established the Salt Lake Forest Reserve in order to protect the surrounding mountains and watershed. Today, Salt Lake City Public Utilities, in collaboration with the US Forest Service, monitor the quality of Salt Lake City's drinking water and educate the public on the best ways to be stewards.

The leading contributors to watershed contamination today are development and recreational use. More than 5 million people visit the watershed canyons in Salt Lake County. Water-borne organisms from domesticated animals and humans flow to the water treatment plant in less than 24 hours. That is why it's critical to respect regulations in the watershed:

- Stay out of the water (no swimming or wading).
- Dogs, and other domesticated animals, are prohibited in watersheds.
- Do not litter. Pack out what you pack in.
- Stay on designated trails.
- Use only bathroom facilities and carry a waste bag for emergencies.
- Observe all posted guidelines.

Hikes in this book that explore Salt Lake County's watershed include trails in Bells Canyon (Hike 28), Big Cottonwood Canyon (Hikes 29–32), Little Cottonwood Canyon (Hikes 33–36), and a portion of Quail Hollow (Hike 25) and City Creek Canyon (Hike 8).

WEATHER AND CLIMATE

Salt Lake genuinely experiences all four seasons, and temperatures can vary over 100 degrees from summer highs to winter lows! Some hikes in this book are inaccessible or best explored during certain periods. The route descriptions include clear notes about prime seasons, if applicable.

Winter. During the winter, temperatures in the city drop well below freezing, and alpine temps dip below 0 degrees Fahrenheit. With snow and ice, trails morph into picturesque winter wonderlands. Make sure to bring appropriate clothing for freezing temperatures, including waterproof outer layers, warm insulating layers (down, fleece, wool), a warm cap, gloves, and quality snow boots, plus micro-traction spikes and hiking poles.

Some of the canyon trails are not appropriate for winter hiking, especially if they move through avalanche terrain. Hiking in avalanche terrain is a serious business and can be fatal—avalanche safety education and equipment (shovel, beacon, probe) are essential. Each hike's information block clearly states if the trail crosses avalanche terrain.

On the flip side, there are dozens of lower-elevation trails, that are most enjoyable with cooler temps.

Spring. Spring is one of the most pleasant times to be in nature. It's terrific to witness flora and fauna waking up from winter's slumber. Blossoms, leaf buds, and migrating birds first appear on the lower-elevation trails. As the days warm, the snow line recedes, and mountains begin to come alive. The foothills flourish first, then the new grasses and wildflowers start to climb, trailing the snowmelt. The highest elevation routes are often inaccessible until the end of spring or the beginning of summer.

Spring can also be very muddy. If the mud is clumping, turn back to ensure the trail's integrity stays intact throughout the warm months.

Summer. Days where the temperature hovers above 100 degrees Fahrenheit are not rare during Salt Lake summers, and they are getting more common as global temperatures continue to rise. Walking unshaded trails on the valley floor in the summer heat isn't much fun and can be dangerous. Additionally, some south- and west-facing lower foothills turn brown and radiate heat during the summer inferno.

However, it's during the warmest months that the high mountain trails genuinely shine. Often when it's over 100 in the valley, the canyons are 10, 20, or 30 degrees cooler. The

Snow-covered trails at Parley's Historic Nature Park (Hike 5)

highlight of high mountain summer hiking is the flora, particularly flowers and blooming shrubs. Prime wildflower season is June through August.

Fall. Autumn is one of the best seasons for hiking in Salt Lake. Cooler temps before the onset of snow make the climate and conditions appropriate for walking most of the trails. The deciduous forests in the canyons and the lush canopy of trees within the city become a kaleidoscope of warm colors.

OUTDOOR ETHICS

The great joy of exploring nature comes with the responsibility to act as stewards. Outdoor ethics means leaving the trail, park, or preserve in as good—or ideally, even better—condition as you found it.

Leave No Trace (LNT) is a nonprofit organization with a mission to "Ensure a sustainable future for the outdoors and the planet." The organization accomplishes its mission by focusing on educating people. Seven LNT principles teach people what it looks like to act as a steward:

1. Plan ahead and prepare
2. Travel and camp on durable surfaces
3. Dispose of waste properly
4. Leave what you find
5. Minimize campfire impacts
6. Respect wildlife
7. Be considerate of others

Obtain additional information and become more familiar with LNT principles at lnt.org.

PACK IT IN, PACK IT OUT

This means everything that comes with you into the natural environment must leave with you as well. Disposing of waste properly (LNT principle 3) takes special consideration and attention. "Everything" includes obvious items like water bottles, micro-trash like slivers of granola bar wrappers, and even biodegradable stuff like orange peels and sandwich crumbs. Better yet, take it one step further and remove waste left behind by less informed users.

WILDERNESS

The National Wilderness Preservation System, established by the Wilderness Act of 1964, is a network of more than 800 federally designated wilderness areas. In these wilderness areas, the land is preserved in its natural condition,

A hiker practices LNT principle #3 by removing waste left behind by others.

and solitude is placed at a premium. Wilderness is protected from development and the incursion of motorized or mechanized equipment. In fact, wilderness areas are spaces where humans can visit for short periods but not remain.

This book features hikes in three wilderness areas: Mount Olympus Wilderness (Hikes 19–21); Twin Peaks Wilderness (Hikes 24 and 29); and Lone Peak Wilderness (Hike 28). When hiking in these places, please practice LNT principles and follow these specific wilderness rules:

- Limit group size to 12, which includes both people and animals.
- No motorized and mechanized equipment of any kind is allowed, including bicycles.
- Observe campfire restrictions and prohibitions.
- Do not cut switchbacks.

TRAIL ETIQUETTE

Being a good steward also means being courteous on the trail. Observing hiking etiquette creates a more enjoyable and safe experience for all users. Here are a few guidelines that lay a foundation for considerate encounters:

- **Observe the right-of-way.** Uphill hikers have the right-of-way because it's hard to regenerate momentum after stopping abruptly on a climb. If you are heading downhill, move aside for uphill hikers. Some of the routes in this book are open to equestrians, mountain bikers, and cyclists. When meeting bicyclists or horseback riders, folks on foot should step aside and let others pass.

- **Move aside for horses.** When encountering a horse, step to the downhill side of the trail (if possible) to avoid spooking the creature. If stepping on the uphill side is necessary, crouch a bit to not tower over the horse's head. Calm the horse by making yourself visible and speaking in a normal voice to the riders. If walking with a dog, keep them under control.

- **Stay on trails.** Avoid the temptation to cut switchbacks or blaze new "shortcuts." The established trail is a durable surface (see LNT principle 2), and choosing to walk on designated trails protects sensitive surroundings by preventing unnecessary environmental degradation.

- **Obey the rules.** As simple as it sounds: observe and respect restrictions for each specific trail and area. In Salt Lake, watershed-based restrictions help keep drinking water safe. Don't bring dogs or other animals into watershed areas, and don't swim in them.

- **Keep dogs under control.** When hiking with the pup, follow the area's leash rules. If dogs are allowed off-leash, ensure they stay on the trail and are under strict voice control. Dog waste is unsightly, smelly, and can spread disease; clean up after your pet.

- **Take only pictures.** Leave pieces of nature in nature. Don't bring home natural elements or historical artifacts. It's especially tempting to pick wildflowers. Refrain from gathering a bouquet or even snatching a single flower. Practice consideration for the creatures who rely on wildflowers for food and leave nature intact for other observers to enjoy (see LNT principles 4 and 7).

WILDLIFE

The variable geography in Salt Lake means the area supports rich biological diversity. It's exciting to see the animals who share our environment, but you should always avoid disturbing wildlife (see LNT principle 6). Watch from a distance and resist the desire to approach or feed wild animals.

No social media photo justifies threatening the well-being of our fellow creatures or yourself.

Docile creatures such as birds, Uinta ground squirrels, foxes, squirrels, chipmunks, gophers, and voles are fun to watch. Typically, large ungulates like deer, elk, and moose are passive and also safe to observe. However, if a moose feels threatened, it will charge.

Moose. Maintaining distance is the best way to avoid irritating a moose. Back off if it shows signs of aggression, like

PLEASE DO NOT FEED THE WILDLIFE

Please do not feed the wildlife. When wild animals eat foreign foods, it disrupts their nutrient intake and digestion, which can be fatal. Dependency on human food can also make animals aggressive. Accustomed to handouts, the Uinta ground squirrels around Lake Blanche will approach within a few feet of picnickers, and the resident foxes at Big Cottonwood Regional Park get far too close. Instead of adding to the problem, enjoy watching these animals eat foods natural to their environment.

snout licking or laying its ears back. Stay calm and do not run away. Talk in a normal voice while slowly backing away in the direction you came. If the moose charges, it's helpful to know they have terrible eyesight. Head for the largest solid object, like a tree, and hide behind it. If you get knocked down, curl into a ball and protect your head.

Omnivorous bears and resident carnivores like coyotes, cougars, and rattlesnakes are typically harmless, only engaging with humans when they feel threatened. Making some noise on the trail can prevent an encounter, but in the event of a confrontation, it's essential to know how to act.

Coyotes. If you encounter a coyote, do not approach. And do not turn your back! Pick up small pets or children. Face the coyote and make loud noises, stomp your feet, or throw rocks and sticks to frighten it away. Wave your arms and back away slowly.

Cougars. Encounters are very rare. If you see a cougar, stop. Never run from a cougar, and do not approach it. Maintain eye contact and pick up small children or pets. Never crouch; stand up tall and wave hiking poles, a jacket, or sticks above your head to appear larger. Talk in a firm, loud voice while backing away slowly. If attacked, fight back with all your strength. If you are aggressive enough, the cougar may flee.

Rattlesnakes. Always wear closed-toed shoes, whether you're hiking in the city or beyond. Prevent an encounter by being observant of your surroundings. Listen for the sound of a rattle and try to locate where it's coming from before moving. Warn other trail users. If you see a rattlesnake, do not poke or touch it. In the event of any snake bite, treat it as if it were venomous. Do not suck out the venom, and do not use a tourniquet. Seek medical attention immediately.

Black bears. Encounters are infrequent. If a black bear stands up, grunts, woofs, moans, or makes sounds, it's not being aggressive. It's trying to get a better look or smell. Stand

Please don't feed the wildlife. The best meal is one that animals forage for themselves.

your ground; do not run or climb a tree. Never back up, lie down, or play dead. Use hiking poles, a jacket, or sticks and wave them above your head to make yourself appear larger. If attacked, use bear spray, or fight back using sticks, rocks, packs, or anything available.

Ticks. These tiny arachnids feed on larger animals and carry diseases that can harm humans, pets, and wildlife. Although most ticks in Utah do not have Lyme disease, it's always a good idea to protect against tick bites. Wear long pants tucked into socks and long-sleeve shirts, and perform tick checks on yourself after your hike. Wash hair and skin thoroughly, and wash clothing in hot water after spending time outdoors.

For more information about how to prevent and manage wildlife encounters, visit wildawareutah.org.

FLORA

Becoming acquainted with regional trees, shrubs, and wild-flowers adds a new layer of enjoyment to wilderness rambles. Use *Urban Trails: Salt Lake City*, including its Guide to Wild-flowers (which identifies a few dozen wildflowers, shrubs, and flowering trees), to explore Salt Lake's flora. You might also consider downloading a plant identification app. Learning the names and characteristics of plants you find along the trail is likely to become a joyous part of your nature excursions.

To accompany this book's Guide to Wildflowers, here are some fun facts about tree species you'll encounter on these hikes:

- **Quaking aspens are the state tree of Utah.** A member of the willow family, their long, slender, white trunks are aesthetic year-round. The namesake leaves quiver in the breeze and, like a musical instrument, create a soothing melody. In autumn, the foliage turns the color of yellow flames and strawberry sunsets.

Fremont cottonwood trees along the Jordan River Parkway (Hike 1)

- **Fremont cottonwoods** are another member of the willow family, with similarly shaped leaves as the quaking aspen.
- **Gambel oaks** are one of the most common trees and can be the size of a bush or dozens of feet tall, depending on their proximity to a water source. They are heat-loving and thrive on south- and west-facing slopes.
- **Bigtooth maples** often grow alongside Gambel oaks near water sources. They can vary significantly in size. During autumn, the leaves turn fire-engine red.
- **Curl-leaf mountain mahogany** is an evergreen shrub or small tree found in dry, arid soils. It's an essential food for deer and other animals during the winter.
- **White pines** make up many of the trees found in coniferous mountain forests. Mature trees can grow up to a hundred feet tall.
- **Rocky Mountain junipers** are evergreen trees with noticeable, bright-blue berry-like cones. They grow in rocky areas.

WATER AND GEAR

While it's possible to experience many of the trails in this book without a lot of preparation or gear, it's always more enjoyable to be prepared. Due to an uptick of interest in light and fast travel, people are getting caught deep in the wilderness without appropriate equipment. The Salt Lake County Sheriff's Search and Rescue team is experiencing a record-breaking number of calls, a staggering amount of them due to people not being prepared (e.g., cold temperatures, feeling too tired to continue). While it's tempting to join the light-and-fast craze and head out with nothing but shoes and the clothes on your back, it's better to avoid becoming a rescue statistic. Put together an easy-to-grab bag that includes the **Ten Essentials**, and bring it with you, even on short outings.

THE TEN ESSENTIALS

The point of the **Ten Essentials**, originated by The Mountaineers, has always been to answer two basic questions: Can you prevent emergencies and respond positively should one occur (items 1–5)? And can you safely spend a night—or more—outside (items 6–10)? Use this list as a guide and tailor it to the needs of your outing.

1. **Navigation.** Carry a map and compass and know how to use them. Download area maps to your cellphone using Gaia, CalTopo, or other mapping applications. Bring an external battery and charging cord for the device.

2. **Headlamp.** Invest in an ultra-light headlamp that takes up very little space. A headlamp can be a lifesaver and is always useful when the sun sets, even on neighborhood strolls.

3. **Sun protection.** Sun gear is particularly important in Salt Lake's year-round sunny climate. A brimmed hat, sunglasses, and sunscreen are a must. A sun hoody or other garment that covers the whole body is the best form of sun protection, especially in the high alpine environment.

4. **First-aid supplies.** A first-aid kit helps ensure minor injuries on the trail stay minor. At a minimum, a first-aid kit includes bandages, gauze, tape, scissors, an elastic bandage for sprains, pain relievers, antiseptics, and medication for allergic reactions.

5. **Knife.** A pocketknife or multitool can come in useful for basic repairs or even picnics.

6. **Fire.** It's very unlikely that a fire will be necessary. However, carrying a few matches or a lighter is wise, in case an emergency requires spending the night outdoors.

7. **Emergency shelter.** This can be as simple as using a trash bag or rain poncho that can double as an emergency tarp.

8. **Nutrition.** Pack enough food for the given objective. Then bring extra for X-factor scenarios. A sleeve of sugar blocks and an energy bar can go a long way.

9. **Hydration.** Always bring water, even for a quick jaunt. During the hot Salt Lake summers, a single person may require up to two gallons of water a day. Water filtration tablets or devices can be useful for hikes near watercourses. During the winter, a thermos of tea or soup can significantly warm up the body.

10. **Insulation.** Weather can change rapidly, and the temperatures in the canyons are drastically different from the valley floor. Always bring more layers than you intend to use.

PERMITS, REGULATIONS, AND PARK FEES

Most trails in this book are managed by city and county municipalities, the US Forest Service, or conservation agencies. There are only two areas that require a fee: Mill Creek Canyon (Hikes 14–17) and Red Butte Garden (Hike 9). Regulations, including dog policies, restrictions, and closures, are specifically indicated in each route's information block.

ROAD AND TRAIL CONDITIONS

Typically, trails don't change much over time. However, significant weather events like avalanches and windstorms can rapidly alter an entire landscape. It's a good idea to contact the relevant land management agency for up-to-date information (see Resources).

Winter and snow alter accessibility to several of the hiking locations. Mill Creek Canyon Road is closed midway up the canyon throughout the winter and into late spring. Utah Department of Transportation (UDOT) often enforces that only all-wheel or 4-wheel-drive vehicles with snow tires can enter Big Cottonwood Canyon and Little Cottonwood Canyon during snowstorms. It's not uncommon for avalanches to hit the road in Little Cottonwood Canyon, and UDOT regularly shuts down the canyon to perform avalanche control work.

HUNTING

The only trail in this book that permits hunting is City Creek Canyon (Hike 8). It's best to check with the Utah Division of Wildlife Resources (wildlife.utah.gov/hunting) for information and City Creek Canyon hunting permits. When hiking during hunting season, wear orange and make yourself visible.

SAFETY CONCERNS

Trails and parks are typically safe places. Common sense and vigilance are still important, however, particularly for solo trail users. If hiking alone, be sure to let someone know where you are and when you expect to be back. Assess the trailhead and surrounding area before heading out. If a person or situation feels suspicious or unsafe, trust your intuition.

Unfortunately, car break-ins are common. Bring valuables like wallets and cell phones along on the walk. Try to leave the car empty and move things like reusable bags out of sight. Sunshades can be useful in deterring interest in your vehicle.

There is a significant homeless population in Salt Lake. Most of the trails in this book avoid homeless encampments, but if it is common in a given area, I note that in the hike description. If you encounter a homeless encampment, keep to yourself, keep moving, stay vigilant, and remember to practice compassion.

FEELING EMPOWERED ON THE TRAIL

Part of the reason I undertook the project of writing this guidebook is that I've experienced how deflating it is to be lost or doubting myself in nature. My husband, who is a certified mountain guide through the American Mountain Guide Association,

Fall colors illuminate Red Butte Garden's botanical walking paths (Hike 9).

always seems so dialed in, and it's easy to take a back seat. Through this project, I've learned a few tricks that help me feel empowered while navigating wild places.

Blue dot navigation is awesome. With mapping applications like Gaia and CalTopo, for a small fee, it's possible to track every movement of a hike. The blue dot on the map (which works for downloaded maps even with no cell phone service) reveals an exact location in reference to other trails and points of interest. It's fun to follow and can prevent you from getting turned around.

A little research can go a long way. Reading about trail conditions, including mileage and elevation, is essential in deciding how much food, water, and clothing are necessary. Planning ahead makes adventuring more fun.

A satellite texting device is a wonderful investment. While they can be a bit spendy, these devices provide peace of mind for wilderness explorations that go outside of cell phone service, especially when hiking solo.

A NOTE ABOUT SAFETY

Safety is an important concern in all outdoor activities. No guidebook can alert you to every hazard or anticipate the limitations of every reader. Therefore, the descriptions of roads, trails, routes, and natural features in this book are not representations that a particular place or excursion will be safe for your party. When you follow any of the routes described in this book, you assume responsibility for your own safety. Under normal conditions, such excursions require the usual attention to traffic, road and trail conditions, weather, terrain, the capabilities of your party, and other factors. Keeping informed on current conditions and exercising common sense are the keys to a safe, enjoyable outing.

—Mountaineers Books

Next page: *Murals along Parley's Trail liven up the cityscape (Hike 4).*

TRANS-CITY TRAILS

The two featured trans-city trails, the Jordan River Parkway (Hike 1) and Parley's Trail (Hike 4), are alluring for several reasons: they connect heavily urban areas with green spaces, they take advantage of human-powered transportation corridors, and they are easy to access via public transit. This last point is particularly significant for Salt Lake, where public transportation doesn't reach many of the surrounding canyons and mountains.

The Jordan River Parkway is part of a collaborative restoration project between the Jordan River Commission and regional land management agencies. The trail extends from Utah Lake to the Great Salt Lake, spanning the entire north-to-south length of Salt Lake County and then some. The Jordan River Parkway passes two exceptional areas. Dozens of migrating bird species flock to the restored wetlands and marshes within the Redwood Nature Area (Hike 2). The paths in Germania Park, Jordan Preserve, and Little Confluence (Hike 3) wander along the banks of the Jordan River amid native foliage and thriving bird populations.

Parley's Trail (Hike 4), managed by Parley's Rails, Trails, and Tunnels (PRATT) Coalition, spans Salt Lake County from east to west. Plans include extending Parley's Trail to connect with the Jordan River Parkway. Parley's Trail links several parks and points of interest, including Parley's Historic Nature Park (Hike 5), where Parleys Creek winds through 88 acres of protected green space, a hub for native plant and animal species. Another notable stop is Sugar House Park (Hike 6), which features astonishing views of the Wasatch along a paved pedestrian route, plus bountiful playgrounds, picnic areas, and sports courts.

1   Jordan River Parkway

DISTANCE:	Up to 35 miles one way
ELEVATION GAIN:	1120 feet
HIGH POINT:	4610 feet
DIFFICULTY:	Easy to moderate
TIME:	30 minutes or more
FITNESS:	Walkers, runners
FAMILY-FRIENDLY:	Yes, the entire trail is paved. Aside from a few steep sections, the route is stroller- and ADA-accessible.
DOG-FRIENDLY:	Yes, on-leash. Poop bags and waste bins throughout.
AMENITIES:	Trailheads, restrooms, drinking water, playgrounds, pavilions, picnic areas, sports courts, maps, interpretive signs, nature centers, fishing
CONTACT/MAP:	Jordan River Commission
GPS:	40.80795˚N, 111.93941˚W
BEFORE YOU GO:	The Jordan River Parkway stretches the entire length of Salt Lake City from north to south. There are more than twenty trailheads in addition to countless parks, nature centers, and sights along the trail. Swimming, wading, and domestic animals are prohibited in the Jordan River.

GETTING THERE

Public Transit: Although there isn't a good public transit option to access the Redwood trailhead (this hike's start), other trail access points can be easily reached by taking TRAX Green Line to Fairpark Station or River Trail Station, TRAX Red Line to Historic Gardner Station, or UTA FrontRunner to Draper Station. **Bike Route:** Use the Salt Lake City & County Bikeways Map to plot a route to the trailhead. **Driving:** To reach the northernmost trailhead in Salt Lake County, from I-215 take exit 23 for 700 N and travel east for 0.5 mile. Turn left on Redwood Road and drive 1.6 miles. The Redwood Road trailhead is on the left.

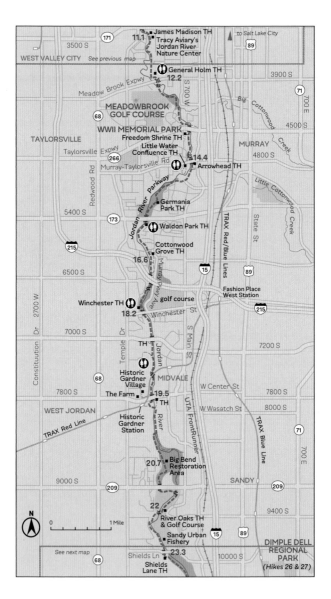

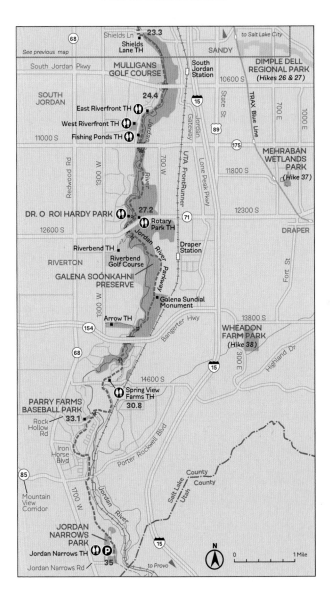

A CORRIDOR OF LIFE

"The Jordan River Corridor will become recognized as a valued regional amenity that brings people together and links them with the natural world, providing unique and memorable experiences for residents and visitors alike. With the Jordan River as its heart, this 50-mile-long greenway will connect the freshwater Utah Lake with the marshlands and saline waters of the vast and scenic Great Salt Lake."

In December of 2008, Blueprint Jordan River completed a visioning process to address the failing ecology around the river. Public input helped establish guiding principles for restoring riparian and in-stream habitats while balancing the needs for development, recreation, and public access. Goals included preserving and rehabilitating natural river features by establishing buffers between the river and the built environment, incorporating natural and cultural history into designs and waterfront features, and connecting communities to the river corridor, with an emphasis on non-automobile travel.

A bridge crosses the Jordan River in the Galena Soónkahni Preserve.

The Jordan River, located between the Wasatch and Oquirrh Mountains, flows north for 50 miles from Utah Lake to the Great Salt Lake. The river is fundamental to maintaining northern Utah's biological diversity and understanding the region's heritage.

Archeological evidence reveals that humans have lived alongside the Jordan River for at least 3000 years. But in just 150 years, between the arrival of pioneers in the mid-1800s and the booming urban growth that began in the early 2000s, the Jordan River's ecological health has become critically compromised. The culprits are excessive urban development, poor stewardship, and the rerouting of channels and canals for agricultural, industrial, and residential use. Fortunately, in 2008, a community action plan was launched to restore the health of the Jordan River (see sidebar).

Since 2010, the Jordan River Commission and regional partners have worked to create a linear nature preserve with mixed-use river centers and environmental education initiatives. The restoration project includes the Jordan River Parkway, a 45-mile-long pedestrian corridor that explores parks, natural areas, and restored riparian habitats. In just over a decade, many acres along the Jordan River have been restored as free-flowing ribbons of life.

With dozens of scenic bridges, underpasses, and resting spots, the Jordan River Parkway could fill a whole book. The portion described here is a 35-mile stretch that starts at the northernmost trailhead in Salt Lake County and ends at the southernmost trailhead in Salt Lake County and is a great choice year-round. The parkway continues to the north and south beyond this description. This suggested route highlights trailheads and points of interest so you can customize your outing. There are countless neighborhood access points and other pedestrian corridor connections, but the detailed signs you'll see on the trail will help you stay on track. The paper or digital map available from the Jordan

River Commission (see Resources) is an invaluable tool for planning and exploring the parkway.

GET MOVING

The first 11 miles create the northern segment of the Jordan River Parkway. This area's highlights include the Fred and Ila Rose Fife Wetland Preserve along the 9-Line Trail, Jordan Park and the peaceful cultural displays of the International Peace Gardens, and educational opportunities at the Tracy Aviary's Jordan River Nature Center.

Begin at the Redwood trailhead, which at 4220 feet is the lowest point of elevation along the trail. From the Jordan River Parkway map sign, cross Redwood Road, and start walking south. You'll find that the first 16 miles are mostly flat, gaining a cumulative 200 or so feet of elevation.

At 1.7 miles, come to a charming nature exploration area with footbridges over marshlands and a vista of Ensign Peak (Hike 7) to the east. Over the next 1.5 miles, there is a dense homeless population, particularly between Riverside Park trailhead (1.9 miles), Cottonwood Park trailhead (2.75 miles), and the Northwest Community and Recreation Center (3.4 miles).

You'll reach the scenic Utah State Fairgrounds (TRAX Green Line, Fairpark) at 3.6 miles, where the homeless population begins to dwindle. Just past the fairgrounds, the route comes to a huge metal pedestrian bridge that crosses a web of railroad tracks. Shortly after the bridge is Alzheimer's Wildlife Grove and trailhead.

At 5.5 miles, the walkway encounters several significant points of interest. After entering the 9th South River Park, there is a junction with the restored wetlands on the 9-Line Trail and the Fred and Ila Rose Fife Wetland Preserve. Past the 9-Line Trail, the parkway meanders along the perimeter of the International Peace Gardens (free admission, open 7:00 AM to 10:00 PM). The peace gardens (which are part of Jordan Park

Mount Olympus and Broads Fork Twin Peaks rise beyond a bridge across the Jordan River.

and trailhead) are indeed a place of serenity. Organized in 1947, this beautifully manicured parcel of land includes monuments and tributes to over two dozen countries.

After the peace gardens, come to Modesto Park at 6.3 miles from the start. The next significant site is the Three Waters Confluence, where Red Butte, Emigration, and Parley's Creeks flow into the Jordan River at the same location. The area was covered with pavement and neglected until it was restored by the Seven Canyons Trust.

At 7.3 miles is 17th South Park leading to Glendale Golf Course. Cross an impressive cement bridge with a pristine view at 8.2 miles and intercept the work-in-progress future connection to Parley's Trail (Hike 4). There is almost no shade for 5 miles after the Glendale Golf Course.

Reach Redwood Trailhead Park (TRAX Green Line, River Trail) at 9 miles (trailhead parking temporarily closed), and look east for a Wasatch panoramic of Grandeur Peak (Hike 15), Neffs Canyon (Hike 19), Mount Olympus (Hike 20), the Broads Fork Twin Peaks, the upper basin of Bells Canyon (Hike 28), and Lone Peak.

The east section of the Redwood Nature Area (Hike 2) is at 9.6 miles. Then at 11.1 miles you'll arrive at James Madison Park and trailhead, featuring Tracy Aviary's Jordan River Nature Center, an educational destination with free admission (open Thursday and Friday from 4:00 PM to 8:00 PM, plus Saturday and Sunday from 8:00 AM to 4:00 PM).

Between 11 and 23 miles is the middle segment of the Jordan River Parkway. This area's highlights include the riparian walking paths around Germania Park and Little Waters Confluence (Hike 3), opportunities to explore the charming shopping and historical center of Gardner Village, and the new habitats being created at Big Bend Restoration Area.

Arriving at General Holm Park and trailhead at 12.2 miles will bring you to a 5-mile stretch of shady patches leading to Germania Park. A half mile past General Holm, the corridor enters a dense canopy of Fremont cottonwood trees in a protected revegetation area. Past the WWII Memorial Park, you'll arrive at the Arrowhead trailhead at 14.4 miles.

The next 1.5 miles between Arrowhead trailhead and Germania Park trailhead (Hike 3) are brimming with beautiful sites and ecological information. Past Germania Park, the grade gets gradually steeper. Reach the Cottonwood Grove trailhead at 16.6 miles, and pass the Murray City Golf Course and Winchester trailhead at 18.2 miles.

Arrive at Historic Gardner Village (TRAX Red Line, Historic Gardner) at 19.5 miles. Gardner Village is a stand-alone destination featuring relics of Utah's pioneering heritage, including a working mill plus restaurants, boutique shopping, entertainment, and The Farm—an animal rescue and petting farm with pony rides.

The route is nearly flat for 9 miles south of Gardner Village, gaining just over 100 feet in elevation, with very few shady sections. At 20.7 miles is the Big Bend Restoration Area, currently under construction. When complete, it will feature a riparian habitat with replanted native flora. The River Oaks trailhead and golf course are at 22 miles, then Shields Lane trailhead at 23.3.

The final 13 miles comprises the southern segment of the Jordan River Parkway. This area's highlight is the 250-acre Galena Soónkahni Preserve, which houses an archeological site with human artifacts that are more than 3000 years old. Within the preserve, the Galena Sundial Monument recognizes eight tribes that lived in the area for centuries before the arrival of pioneers.

Across 10600 South from Mulligans Golf Course, at 24.4 miles, is a commercial center where you'll find snacks and libations. Between 25 and 27.2 miles you'll encounter the East Riverfront, West Riverfront, and Fishing Ponds trailheads and Dr. O Roi Hardy Park.

At 28.2 miles, enter the 250-acre Galena Soónkahni Preserve, a historical and ecological treasure along the Jordan River (FrontRunner, Draper). Native plants like big sage, rubber rabbitbrush, and cattails fill the landscape. An archeological site within the preserve contains human artifacts more than 3000 years old.

The parkway continues for just under 2 miles within the preserve. About halfway through is the Galena Sundial Monument, which recognizes eight tribes that inhabited the area for centuries before the arrival of homesteaders. From the monument, Lone Peak and Mount Timpanogos crown the eastern skyline.

Past the monument is a hill with a steep grade. Then the trail begins to vary more drastically in steepness for the remaining 6 miles as you pass the Spring View Farms trailhead at 30.8 miles and the Parry Farms Baseball Park at 33.1 miles. You'll arrive at Jordan Narrows, the final trailhead in Salt Lake County, 35 miles from the northern trailhead and the trail's highest point of elevation, 4610 feet. The Jordan River Parkway continues for 10 miles into Utah County.

GO FURTHER

The Jordan River Commission hosts Love Your Watershed on the second Saturday of every month. During the monthly gathering, participants spend a few hours helping with clean-up and restoration along the Jordan River. Love Your Watershed is a perfect outlet for folks seeking to become better stewards.

2 Redwood Nature Area and Decker Lake

DISTANCE:	4.5 miles
ELEVATION GAIN:	50 feet
HIGH POINT:	4250 feet
DIFFICULTY:	Easy
TIME:	3 hours
FITNESS:	Walkers, runners
FAMILY-FRIENDLY:	Yes, paved trails around Redwood Nature Area are stroller- and ADA-accessible. Busy road crossing.
DOG-FRIENDLY:	Yes, on-leash. Waste bin at Lester Street trailhead.
AMENITIES:	Restrooms, benches, sports fields, interpretive signs, drinking water
CONTACT/MAP:	Jordan River Commission; Salt Lake County Parks and Open Space
GPS:	40.70490˚N, 111.93601˚W
BEFORE YOU GO:	There is little shade on the Cross Towne Trail and around Decker Lake.

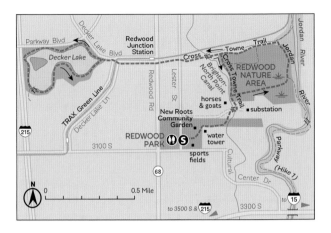

GETTING THERE

Public Transit: Take TRAX Green Line to Redwood Junction Station. Start the route on the Cross Towne Trail, parallel to the TRAX. **Bike Route:** Use the Salt Lake City & County Bikeways Map to plot a route to the trailhead. **Driving:** From I-15, take exit 303 for UT 171 / 3300 S. Go west on 3300 S for 1.2 miles. Turn right on Cultural Center Drive for 0.5 mile. At the roundabout, take the second exit onto 3100 S / Rosa Parks Drive, and travel for 0.3 mile. Turn right on Lester Street and immediately right into the parking lot at Redwood Park.

This hike meanders around the Redwood Nature Area, then uses the Cross Towne Trail to circumnavigate Decker Lake, a popular park with tall grasses, waterfowl, and mountain views. The natural area and extended walking paths are a great destination for birders, families, and dog walkers, and it's a space well enjoyed by the surrounding community of residents and office workers.

The 63-acre Redwood Nature Area is part of a web of restored natural habitats along the Jordan River. Until 2008, the area was a fill site for dredged sediment, and a grazing ground for livestock, and it was entangled with invasive plant species like Russian olive, tamarisk, and puncture vine.

A restoration team and volunteers meticulously removed the thriving invasive plant species and re-created a wetland habitat by installing culverts that redirect water from the Brighton–North Point Canal and the Jordan River. The team then reseeded the re-created riparian area with native bulrush, sedges, and saltgrass.

Today the Redwood Nature Area is flourishing with native trees, such as willows, box elders, poplars, and cottonwoods. The reclaimed wetlands are a vital habitat for more than 130 bird species, including blue herons, American avocets, chickadees, yellow-headed blackbirds, and lesser yellowlegs. The sanctuary is also home to red foxes and boreal chorus frogs.

GET MOVING

From the map kiosk at the parking area, begin walking on the paved pathway toward the water tower. Skirt between the tower and the New Roots Refugee Community Garden, following the trail as it veers right to the Brighton–North Point Canal. At 0.3 mile, the path reaches a dirt road. Go right and cross the Brighton–North Point Canal on a bridge. There is a large substation in front of you, but don't worry, the path quickly passes the buzzing electrical currents.

Follow the trail to the left along the canal and say hello to the horses and goats on the other side. A half mile from the start, the route comes to the perimeter of the Redwood Nature Area and splits. Turn right to begin the nature area loop. The restored wetland environment soon becomes visible on both sides of the path, and benches and mature trees make this an ideal spot to linger and listen to the wildlife attracted to the riparian habitat.

At 0.8 mile, the route veers left onto the Jordan River Parkway (Hike 1) for a short distance alongside a lively seasonal

Decker Lake sits on the edge of an office park and sports eastern views of snow-capped Wasatch peaks.

bird pond. On a clear day, the Oquirrh Mountains form a gorgeous backdrop across the pond.

The next junction is the Cross Towne Trail. Turn left and enjoy the scattered shade of mature trees as you continue to loop around the preserve. At 1.4 miles, where the walkway forks at a grove of white poplars, you have a choice: continue straight to reach Decker Lake, or shorten your walk to 1.9 miles by turning left and returning to the trailhead.

To reach Decker Lake, stay on the Cross Towne Trail and cross the Brighton-North Point Canal again. Exit the Redwood Nature Area and follow the alley parallel to the TRAX, making sure to take care when crossing Lester Street and busy Redwood Road.

Pass by the TRAX Redwood Junction Station (public transportation start) and reach Decker Lake 2 miles from the trailhead. Decker Lake is a well-liked park for families and dog walkers and rewards visitors with spectacular views of the Wasatch Mountains to the east, with Grandview Peak to the north and Lone Peak to the south. When the sidewalk turns into a paved pedestrian walkway, veer right to begin the loop around the lake, staying on the main path as it hugs the shore.

The course moves over a bridge at 2.4 miles and turns from pavement to gravel. Although the west portion of the lake is noisy from I-215 traffic, the sound quickly dissipates and is replaced by the calls of seagulls, Canada geese, and mallards.

After rounding the lake, return on the Cross Towne Trail until you reach the junction at the white poplar trees. This time, turn right, walking along the canal until you reach the substation and the return path back to the trailhead to complete the 4.5-mile journey.

GO FURTHER

Redwood Nature Area and Decker Lake are important information sources for bird researchers. Observations from the world's largest citizen-science database, eBird.org, provide critical data about migrating and residential bird species in the area. Consider downloading a bird identification app to make identifying birds easy and fun.

3

Germania Park and Little Confluence

DISTANCE:	3-mile loop
ELEVATION GAIN:	60 feet
HIGH POINT:	4270 feet
DIFFICULTY:	Easy
TIME:	2 hours
FITNESS:	Walkers, hikers, runners
FAMILY-FRIENDLY:	Yes, some paths are stroller- and ADA-accessible. Places for picnics and nature observation.
DOG-FRIENDLY:	Yes, on-leash. Poop bags and waste bins at Little Confluence trailhead, Arrowhead trailhead, and Germania trailhead. Millrace Park (see Go Farther) has an off-leash dog park (permit required).
AMENITIES:	Parking, restrooms, drinking water, interpretive signs, pavilions, picnic benches, BBQ grills, sports field, playgrounds, fishing pond
CONTACT/MAP:	Murray City Parks and Recreation; Taylorsville Parks and Recreation
GPS:	40.65387°N, 111.92230°W
BEFORE YOU GO:	Jordan River Trail hours are 5:00 AM to 11:00 PM. No swimming and no dogs in the river. Although there are patches of shade, some exposed sections can be hot in summer. An excellent winter hike.

GETTING THERE

Public Transit: Take UTA bus route 54 and get off at 5400 S / 1070 W on the corner of Riverside Drive and 5400 S. The trailhead is a few hundred feet north on Riverside Drive. **Bike Route:** Use the Salt Lake City & County Bikeways Map to plot a route to the trailhead. **Driving:** From I-15, take exit 300 for UT 173/5300 S and travel west for 3 miles. Turn right on Riverside Drive; the parking lot is immediately to the left.

This gentle wander is perfect for nature lovers. Belted kingfishers, American goldfinches, black-capped chickadees, spotted

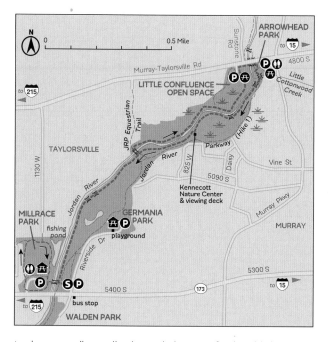

towhees, quails, mallards, and dozens of other bird species harmonize to compose a soothing avian ballad. Beginning at Germania Park's southern trailhead, explore walkways along restored portions of the Jordan River. Meander through a web of footpaths, parks, and natural areas, where flowering shrubs like red-osier dogwood, chokecherry, and Woods' rose combine with sticky purple geranium and Lewis flax to paint the land-scape with a rainbow of new life in the spring and early summer.

Salt Lake County's watershed restoration program is suc-cessfully renewing the stream and riparian habitat between Germania Park, Little Confluence, and Arrowhead Park. Using natural channel design, among other techniques, the water-shed restoration team is seeking to return the Jordan River to its self-sustaining form. Stream renovation projects include riverbank reconstruction, invasive plant removal, and replanting native trees, shrubs, flowers, and grasses.

Murray Parks and Recreation oversees the trailhead, Germania Park, and Arrowhead Park. Taylorsville Parks and Recreation manages Little Confluence trailhead and Millrace Park.

GET MOVING

Locate the starting point near the Jordan River Parkway map, and walk down a short cement path. A bridge straight ahead leads to Millrace Park (see Go Farther). To continue on the main route, don't cross the bridge but instead turn right on the wide dirt path between the paved Jordan River Parkway (Hike 1) and the Jordan River. The next half mile is the most exposed part of the hike, but it passes several shady reprieves with benches.

After 0.4 mile, cross a pair of small footbridges. As the path skirts the byways of Germania Park, keep left to stay on the trail nearest the river. At 0.7 mile, reach the JRP Equestrian Trail junction. Turn left and cross over the Jordan River on a wide bridge, and immediately after, take the narrow dirt footpath to the right.

Begin meandering through the Little Confluence Open Space, watching for interpretive signs. Keep veering right to stay on the trail parallel to the river and avoid turning on the myriad unofficial paths among the trees.

Wander under a luscious canopy of native Fremont cottonwoods, box elders, and invasive Siberian elm and Russian olive. Tamarisk, big sage, narrowleaf willow, and common reeds fill the understory. During late spring, summer, and fall, the dense vegetation erupts with a plethora of color. Just before the trail forks at 1.1 miles, the track narrows and hugs the edge of the Jordan River.

Go right at the fork to continue traversing along the water. After a few hundred feet, the dirt path turns into a gravel

Kennecott Nature Center has built an outdoor classroom along the Jordan River.

road. Follow the road to the Little Confluence trailhead, which marks the convergence of Little Cottonwood Creek and the Jordan River. Walk through the Little Confluence trailhead parking lot toward 4800 South.

At 1.4 miles from the start, turn right onto the 4800 South sidewalk, cross the Jordan River, and turn right toward the Arrowhead Park trailhead. Once in Arrowhead Park, go right when the sidewalk splits to pass peaceful benches overlooking the river and parkway. When the pathway reaches a T intersection, turn right to cross Little Cottonwood Creek on a wooden bridge.

When the path forks at 1.6 miles, go right to roam the well-shaded and secluded restoration area (the elevated boardwalk to the left is the Jordan River Parkway, Hike 1). Cross a small footbridge and keep veering right to stay on the path closest to the river. Encounter another footbridge at 1.8 miles and continue trending right.

You'll see the Kennecott Nature Center outdoor classroom and viewing deck just ahead at 2 miles. Go left to traverse through the outdoor classroom (as long as the school isn't in session) and ascend the stairs to reach the viewing deck platform. Take a moment to soak in the stunning mountain scene, splashy streamside life, and intricate symphony of birdsongs.

Descend the steps to continue the trail, turning left to rejoin the dirt path. Over the next 0.3 mile, continue trending right to stay on the riparian walkway. Pass a riverside beach, then intersect the JRP Equestrian Trail at 2.3 miles, with a familiar bridge to the right. Go straight to retrace the route to the trailhead and complete the 3-mile loop.

GO FARTHER

Walk the paved loop around Millrace Park for a bonus 0.75-mile jaunt. Cross the Jordan River on the bridge opposite the trailhead parking lot and go left to begin a clockwise loop. Avoid the neighborhood exits, staying on the wide, paved trail that hugs the perimeter of the park.

Relish the expansive Wasatch peak views to the east and look for Grandeur Peak (Hike 15), Mount Olympus (Hike 20), Heughs Canyon (Hike 21), and Bells Canyon (Hike 28). At 0.75 mile, complete the loop, crossing the bridge again to return to the trailhead.

4   Parley's Trail

DISTANCE:	6.2 miles one way
ELEVATION GAIN:	840 feet
HIGH POINT:	4930 feet
DIFFICULTY:	Easy to moderate
TIME:	3 hours
FITNESS:	Walkers, runners
FAMILY-FRIENDLY:	The whole route is paved, and the trail west of Sugar House Park is an even grade, making it stroller- and ADA-accessible. However, the trail crosses many streets, some of them busy, and the eastern section has steep hills.
DOG-FRIENDLY:	Yes, on-leash. Poop bags and waste bins throughout.
AMENITIES:	Parking. Additional facilities at Tanner Park, Sugar House Park, and Fairmont Park: restrooms, drinking water, playgrounds, sports courts, picnic tables, pavilions
CONTACT/MAP:	Parley's Rails, Trails, and Tunnels (PRATT) Coalition; Salt Lake County Parks and Open Space
GPS:	40.70747˚N, 111.79593˚W
BEFORE YOU GO:	Parley's Crossing trailhead is open from 7:00 AM to 10:00 PM. After 10:00 PM, the gate closes and the remaining vehicles are towed.

GETTING THERE

Public Transit: Take TRAX S-Line to Fairmont Station. Parley's Trail runs parallel to the TRAX from Fairmont Station to the end

Colorful murals are featured on industrial buildings along Parley's Trail.

of the route. Along the 1.8 miles west of Fairmont Station, Parley's Trail passes five additional S-Line stops. **Bike Route:** Use the Salt Lake City & County Bikeways Map to plot a route to the trailhead. **Driving:** From I-215, take exit 3 for UT 171 S / Wasatch Boulevard / 3300 S and go east. Wasatch Boulevard / 3300 S immediately curves left. Follow the road for half a mile until it dead-ends at the Parley's Crossing trailhead. For a car shuttle, park at Fairmont Park. After completing the hike, take the TRAX S-Line from South Salt Lake Station to Fairmont Station.

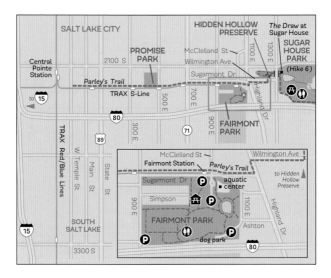

Parley's Trail is a perfect place to enjoy a bit of exercise while shopping or dining in and around Sugar House. And it's one of the only east-west, cross-town, multiuse trails, connecting multiple city parks through a heavily urban environment. Using a bike to connect points of interest is easy and could make for an exciting metro adventure.

You can follow the paved, multiuse trail all the way from Parley's Historic Nature Park (Hike 5) to Sugar House Park (Hike 6) to Hidden Hollow Preserve (Hike 6, Go Farther) to Fairmont Park. A 12-plus-mile roundtrip walk might be too ambitious for most, so the route described here is one-way, starting at the eastern trailhead and finishing on West Temple.

Alternate options include a 3-mile round-trip journey past the historical exhibits at Parley's Nature Park (Hike 5) to the open fields of Tanner Park, or a 7-mile round-trip trek from the trailhead to the peaceful grounds of Sugar House Park (Hike 6). For folks using public transportation, ride to South

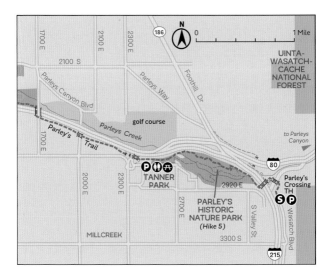

Salt Lake Station and walk east for 2 miles on flat trails past three gorgeous murals to Fairmont Park.

Salt Lake County's goal is to use Parley's Tail to connect the Jordan River Parkway Trail with the Bonneville Shoreline Trail and other Wasatch Range hiking trails. The proposed Parley's Trail, still under construction, continues past West Temple to the Jordan River Parkway (Hike 1). There is no winter management, so there may be snow on the trail in the cold months. Parley's Trail has very little shade, though there is plenty of shade at the parks, and the pavement makes it a good walking option when the season is muddy and temps are cold.

GET MOVING

From the Parley's Crossing trailhead, locate the fence and entrance to Parley's Trail in the southwest corner of the parking lot. At 4930 feet, the trailhead is the highest point of elevation, and the portion of the trail between here and Sugar

House Park is the steepest part of the route, dropping almost 500 feet in 3 miles.

Follow the trail north and cross a connector to I-80 on an overpass at 0.1 mile. The path soon forks: go straight to cross I-215 on another overpass and begin an 11 percent grade descent as you approach Parley's Historic Nature Park (Hike 5). At 0.75 mile, look for the first of four dirt paths on the left that lead into the park. Enjoy the view as it reveals a lush ribbon of life growing around Parleys Creek.

Pass several historical sites 0.8 mile from the trailhead (see Hike 5 for more information). At 1.4 miles, Parleys Trail approaches the east end of Tanner Park, a 10-acre green space with a shady playground and tennis courts. After the park, look north for a sweeping vista of the Capitol Building and downtown. When the pedestrian route forks at 1.8 miles, turn right onto an overpass and then continue through an underpass a short while later. For the next half mile, the way runs close to I-80 and can be noisy.

At 2.5 miles, cross 2000 East on an overpass. Then at 3 miles, Parley's Trail turns to the sidewalk for several hundred feet. Go right on 1700 East to cross I-80 on an overpass and take the next possible left onto the paved pedestrian way.

Here Parley's Trail enters the east side of Sugar House Park (Hike 6) and moves along the park's southern perimeter. The grade mellows out, and the trail's character changes as it winds under mature trees and past grass fields, pavilions, and playgrounds. Follow the path as it veers right, parallel to 1300 East, and at 3.75 miles, cross Parleys Creek when it goes under the sidewalk.

At 3.9 miles, the footpath comes to a significant point of interest along Parley's Trail, *Sego Lily* plaza, a part of *The Draw* at Sugar House (see sidebar). Immediately after *Sego Lily*, follow the way to an underpass below 1300 East to a continuation of *The Draw*. The trail veers left, and at 4 miles from the trailhead, cross Parleys Creek on a wood footbridge at the entrance to Hidden Hollow Preserve (Hike 6, Go Farther).

After the bridge, go left and follow the green-painted path to Wilmington Avenue. The next 0.4 mile of Parley's Trail uses sidewalks until it re-connects with the paved pedestrian pathway at the start of the TRAX S-Line. Turn right on Wilmington Avenue and walk 0.2 mile. Then turn left on Highland Drive, followed by a right on Sugarmont Drive.

At 4.4 miles from the start, cross McClelland Street and encounter the beginning of the TRAX S-Line, the public transportation start. Fairmont Park lies to the south of the TRAX station (see Go Farther).

Parley's Trail runs parallel to the TRAX for the next 1.8 miles. It's almost flat, gradually losing 110 feet of elevation, and native, drought-resistant shrubs like ninebark, shrubby cinquefoil, and red-osier dogwood line the walkway. There are sections of tree-lined walking paths on the south side of the tracks.

Promise Park, a pocket outdoor gym, pops up at 5.3 miles. Just before and after the little park, colorful murals featuring lifelike characters, fantastic creatures, and bold geometric shapes give the industrial buildings some personality.

Russian sage and sunflowers line the path as it traverses residential and industrial zones over the next 0.9 mile. Just before State Street, look for an American Indian and Union Pacific Railroad commemorative mural. The trail continues for another 0.3 mile until it ends at West Temple, 6.2 miles from the trailhead.

GO FARTHER

Explore Fairmont Park, featuring a delightful and shady 1-mile walking loop, an aquatic center, pavilions, a playground, a skate park, restrooms, and an off-leash dog park. The pond behind the aquatic center has beautiful wood boardwalks and plenty of shady benches for bird-watching.

THE DRAW AT SUGAR HOUSE

The Draw at Sugar House is a design by artist Patricia Johanson that combines engineering, landscaping, sculpture, wildlife habitat, flood control, and an outdoor classroom into one inspirational structure.

Part of *The Draw* at Sugar House is the *Sego Lily*, a sandstone-looking formation shaped like Utah's state flower, the sego lily. Each of the three petals has a function beyond pleasing aesthetics. The eastern lily petal represents City Creek Canyon, Red Butte Canyon, Emigration Canyon, Parleys Canyon, Mill Creek Canyon, Big Cottonwood Canyon, and Little Cottonwood Canyon—the seven major Wasatch drainages into the Jordan River. The north petal is a functioning dam that redirects floodwater from 1300 East into Parley's Creek. The west petal features quaint, winding walking paths with viewpoints of the Wasatch Mountains.

The Draw continues past the 1300 East underpass to a sandstone-like slot canyon designed to imitate Echo Canyon, the area the Mormon pioneers witnessed during their initial approach to Utah.

The eastern petal of the Sego Lily *is lined with black-eyed Susans at* The Draw *at Sugar House.*

5 Parley's Historic Nature Park

DISTANCE:	2.4 miles
ELEVATION GAIN:	270 feet
HIGH POINT:	4720 feet
DIFFICULTY:	Easy to moderate
TIME:	1.5 hours
FITNESS:	Walkers, hikers, runners
FAMILY-FRIENDLY:	Yes
DOG-FRIENDLY:	Yes, on-leash in Tanner Park, Parley's Trail, and parking areas. Off-leash on designated trails in Parley's Historic Nature Park. Dogs are prohibited in the protected nature area (see Go Farther). Poop bags and waste bins at east and west parking lots.
AMENITIES:	Parking, restrooms, picnic tables, pavilions, tennis courts, baseball diamond, playground, interpretive signs, historical sites
CONTACT/MAP:	Salt Lake County Parks and Open Space
GPS:	40.71147°N, 111.81801°N
BEFORE YOU GO:	Parley's Historic Nature Park is open from 5:00 AM to 11:00 PM. The off-leash trails make this area a popular choice with dog owners. For people with dog sensitivities, stick to the protected nature area.

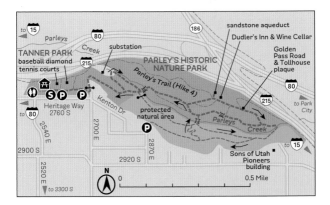

GETTING THERE

Public Transit: Taking public transportation adds 1 mile of walking each way. Take UTA bus route 33 and get off at 3300 S / 2608 E. Travel north on 2600 E for 0.4 mile. Turn left on 3020 S, followed by a right on the next street, 2520 E, and walk for 0.2 mile. Then go right on 2900 S, followed by an immediate left on 2540 E. After 0.2 mile, intercept Heritage Way, turn right, and find the Tanner Park parking area on the left.
Bike Route: Use the Salt Lake City & County Bikeways Map to plot a route to the trailhead. **Driving:** From I-80, take exit 127 toward 2300 E and travel 0.2 mile. At the traffic circle, take the third exit onto 2760 E / Heritage Way and continue for 0.3 mile. The Tanner Park parking area is on the left.

Established in 1986, Parley's Historic Nature Park is 88 acres of green space and riparian habitat, with Parleys Creek at its heart. The creek is the lifeblood of the natural area, nurturing many native species: grasses, willows, and cottonwoods grow in abundance along the water. The robust flora provides food for bats, songbirds, rabbits, and squirrels, which in turn feed larger creatures like red foxes, great-horned owls, Cooper's hawks, and the long-tailed weasel. Parleys Creek is also a habitat for Utah's state fish, the Bonneville cutthroat trout, as well as reptiles and amphibians like tiger salamanders.

In the 1970s, the area was endangered by residential development. Strong opposition from the public encouraged Salt Lake City to acquire the land, parcel by parcel, to preserve it as open space. Thanks to the city's foresight, the area is now a well-loved destination with a flourishing ecosystem.

The trail as described here explores the dog-friendly zones of Parley's Historic Nature Park, as well as a historical section of Parley's Trail. The Go Farther route tours the part of the nature area where dogs are not allowed. During cold and snowy months, the trail can be incredibly slick: micro-traction spikes and poles are helpful. There are meandering byways in the area, and the main track is consistently well-worn.

GET MOVING

The route begins at the west parking area for Tanner Park. Locate the sidewalk and head east, passing tennis courts and a baseball diamond on the left. Just past the baseball diamond, the sidewalk forks; go straight to ascend a short hill. The sidewalk leads to the high point, 4720 feet, which is the east parking lot.

From here, the entrance gate to Parley's Historic Nature Park is within view. Enter the preserve through the gate. The first several hundred feet of the trail are paved, then it turns to a dirt access road. The steepest section of the walk is the initial descent, losing 100 feet of elevation in the first 0.4 mile.

When the grade starts to mellow out, look for a fork in the track, and go left. At 0.5 mile, the route passes a substation on the left. Turn right, and after a few hundred feet, reach the lowest point of elevation at 4600 feet as the walkway meanders next to the rich riparian habitat of Parleys Creek. More than one hundred bird species live in Parley's Historic Nature Park, and this is an excellent location to pull out an identification guide and listen for bird calls.

Before the route intercepts another trail, pass a dog hot spot where canines frolic in the water, then go left to cross a bridge 0.7 mile from the start. When the trail forks again, go left. The dirt path opens to a large meadow with views of Grandeur Peak (Hike 15) straight ahead and Mount Olympus (Hike 20) to the right. When the trail encounters other paths, stay left until you reach the paved Parley's Trail (Hike 4, on-leash area).

Directly ahead is a historical sandstone wall and aqueduct, constructed in 1888 to provide water to Salt Lake's growing population. Cross Parley's Trail to read the plaque and take a closer look at the beautiful masonry. After investigating

Views reach to the north slopes of Grandeur Peak from the protected nature area.

the aqueduct, walk back to Parley's Trail and turn left. At just over a mile from the start, encounter the ruins of Dudler's Inn and Wine Cellar on the left. All that remains of Joseph Dudler's mid-1800s inn, brewery, and saloon are the foundation stones, a crumbling rock wall, and the blocked-off entrance to the wine cellar—a rectangular room with a ten-foot-high rock ceiling.

Continue on Parley's Trail until, at 1.2 miles, it intercepts a dirt trail. Turn right off the pavement to enter Parley's Historic Nature Park again. Walk past the Golden Pass Road and

Tollhouse plaque, which pays homage to the first transportation corridor through Parleys Canyon. The dirt road, constructed by Parley P. Pratt, opened on July 4, 1850, and users were required to pay a toll to help reimburse Pratt for the cost of construction. The Sons of Utah Pioneers building, visible directly ahead, was the site of the original tollhouse.

Veer right and down. When the trail forks, go left toward the Parleys Creek outlet, 1.3 miles from the start. Take a moment to watch the happy dogs cavorting in the water before beginning back.

Retrace the path for a few hundred feet and go left at the junction. The passage leads to a wide clearing. Keep veering left, and at 1.6 miles, cross a bridge. Shortly after, a side path to the left leads to a quaint wood footbridge crossing into the nature area (no dogs). Continue straight, and at the next fork, go right, then veer left. At 1.9 miles, cross the first bridge for a second time, and turn left. The gate to the protected nature area (see Go Farther) is on the left after a few paces. At 2 miles, intercept the route and follow it back to the trailhead to complete the 2.4-mile trip.

GO FARTHER

Parley's Historic Nature Park features a protected nature area that is teeming with wildlife. Dogs are prohibited in order to protect the habitat of ground-nesting and ground-foraging birds.

The natural area loop adds about 2 miles to the route. Enter the western gate and walk on a narrow dirt path as it moves parallel to Parleys Creek. Pass a BMX park and continue trending left until the trail ends at Parleys Creek outlet.

Head back and continue to trend left to create a loop within the nature area. At 0.9 mile, go left at the fork. Ascend a short, steep hill and follow the path to a small trailhead for the nature park (elevation 4780 feet). Turn back here; when the trail forks, go left and drop altitude. Intercept the in-track again, go left, and retrace your steps to the parking lot.

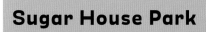

6   Sugar House Park

DISTANCE:	1.8-mile loop
ELEVATION GAIN:	100 feet
HIGH POINT:	4470 feet
DIFFICULTY:	Easy
TIME:	50 minutes
FITNESS:	Walkers, runners
FAMILY-FRIENDLY:	Yes, paved trails are stroller- and ADA-accessible.
DOG-FRIENDLY:	Yes, on-leash
AMENITIES:	Restrooms, pavilions, picnic tables, BBQ grills, water, playgrounds, sports courts
CONTACT/MAP:	Salt Lake County Parks and Open Space
GPS:	40.7318°N, 111.8360°W
BEFORE YOU GO:	Open year-round from dawn to dusk. The park is busiest on weekends. The multiuse path sees diverse users, from walkers and runners to bikers and roller skaters.

GETTING THERE

Public Transit: Take UTA bus route 21 to 2100 S / 1500 E (if you took a westbound bus, walk south to cross 2100 S). The bus stop is at the north entrance of Sugar House Park; begin your loop from there. **Bike Route:** Use the Salt Lake City & County Bikeways Map to plot a route to the trailhead. **Driving:** From I-80, take exit 126 for 1300 E, and go north for 0.3 mile. Turn right on 2100 S and look for the park entrance to the right on 1500 E. Enter the park and follow the one-way road for 0.2 mile. Just before the pond, turn left toward the Big Field Pavilion parking area. If the lot is full, there is parking along the road and at six additional parking lots inside the park.

Sugar House Park is the crown jewel of this historical area, first established in the 1850s by The Church of Jesus Christ of Latter-day Saints settlers. Once an industry hub for ice, coal, lumber, and its namesake sugar beets, the area was also home

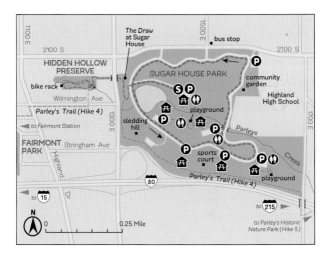

to the Sugar House Jail. By the 1950s, these industries were gone, and the Sugar House neighborhood blossomed into the vibrant shopping area you see today. In 1951, the jail relocated to Draper, leaving an open space that eventually became Highland High School and the 110-acre Sugar House Park.

Sugar House Park is ideal for both sweating and relaxing, with multiple pavilions, BBQ grills, playgrounds, and sports courts. There are many pleasant places to stop for a picnic or pause to soak in mountain views. Flowering trees and towering conifers surround an expansive open area with stunning views of Gobblers Knob, Triangle Peak, Mount Olympus (Hike 20), Broads Fork Twin Peaks, Lone Peak, and the Pfeifferhorn, giving weight to the park's crown jewel claim.

GET MOVING

From the parking area, head west past the pond and connect with the main route in 0.2 mile. The wide, paved, 1.4-mile pedestrian path loops around the park's perimeter, just next to the one-way road. Go left to begin a counter-clockwise loop.

Lovebirds gaze at the impressive Wasatch panorama.

As you begin the loop, the pond is on your left, and you'll see a grassy knoll on the right, which becomes a well-loved sledding hill in the winter. The trail trends southeast, with pavilions, picnic areas, and sports courts on either side.

The path crosses a bridge over Parley's Creek at 0.9 mile, an excellent location to admire the mature box elder and cottonwood trees growing along the stream. Past the bridge, the trail gently ascends through stands of blue spruce, Oregon crab apple, and black walnut trees.

Encounter a community garden on the right, 0.2 mile past the bridge. During the growing season, park-goers can pick any produce growing outside the fenced area. A few hundred feet past the community garden, reach the high point of the hike at 4470 feet. Continue on the path as it veers left.

This north section is a delight in the spring as deciduous trees burst forth in fragrant blooms, painting the sky with pinks, whites, reds, and purples. Several benches invite you to stop and take in the panoramic mountain views.

The trail eventually trends left again, and at 1.6 miles, meets the road leading to the Big Field Pavilion parking area. Turn left to return to the start.

GO FARTHER

An inspirational visit to Hidden Hollow Preserve is the best way to complement a trip to Sugar House Park. The story of the preserve is a moving tale.

In the 1980s, the area was a neglected dumping ground destined to become a parking lot. In 1990, Hawthorn Elementary students from a group called Kids Organized to Protect Our Environment (KOPE) discovered the area, recognized the wilderness potential, and named it Hidden Hollow. Through KOPE, the children mobilized students and families from several elementary schools to rezone Hidden Hollow as an open space. Combining grants and donations with good old-fashioned hard work, they removed 17,602 tons of debris and planted native vegetation.

Permanently protected from encroaching development in 2000, Hidden Hollow Preserve is a sliver of wilderness bounty. The paths roam beneath a canopy of bigtooth maple, box elder, peachleaf willow, pinyon pine, and Gambel oak. The interpretive signs and benches encourage contemplation and appreciation for nature's abundance.

Exploring the preserve adds slightly more than a mile to the Sugar House Park loop. At the end of the loop, instead of turning left and returning to the Big Field Pavilion parking area, cross the park road and locate a sidewalk to the right. When the sidewalk meets a T intersection, go right to follow the path to *The Draw* at Sugar House (see Hike 4 sidebar). Then travel through an underpass. The pathway heads west, with a red rock replica to the left and native shrubs to the right. Follow the path as it veers left to reach a sugar-beet sculpture, then cross a bridge over Parleys Creek and enter the preserve. Go right to begin the 0.2-mile loop. When you arrive back at the bridge, retrace your steps to return to Sugar House Park.

Next page: *Hills of arrowleaf balsamroot above Salt Lake City (Hike 7)*

SALT LAKE CITY

Many of Salt Lake's most treasured nature access zones and green spaces are also within the densest population areas. What's most impressive is that several of these sanctuaries have been giving residents a reprieve from the demands of urban life for over a century. The hike through Memory Park Grove and City Creek Canyon (Hike 8), which begins near the hustle and bustle of the Capitol Building, quickly leads to quiet trails traversing grassy slopes and peaceful woods, with plenty of places to relax along City Creek. Liberty Park (Hike 12), the oldest park in Salt Lake City, is another tranquil space, where enormous trees surround bountiful opportunities for play, picnics, or rest.

This section explores trails around the Utah State Capitol building and the University of Utah's Red Butte Garden (Hike 9). You'll also find wild havens nestled in neighborhoods with free-flowing streams and rich riparian habitats such as Wasatch Hollow Preserve (Hike 13) and Miller Bird Refuge and Bonneville Glen (Hike 11).

One of the best features of the trails in Salt Lake City proper is that they are accessible via public transportation, which will become increasingly important over the next several decades as Salt Lake's growing population continues to be problematic. These treasured spaces are vital nature access points that simultaneously protect wild areas from industrial and residential expansion.

7

Ensign Peak and Nature Park

DISTANCE:	4-mile loop
ELEVATION GAIN:	1320 feet
HIGH POINT:	6150 feet
DIFFICULTY:	Challenging
TIME:	2.5 hours
FITNESS:	Hikers
FAMILY-FRIENDLY:	No, the trail is very steep. An abridged option for children is hiking to the Ensign Peak Monument, 0.5 mile from the trailhead.
DOG-FRIENDLY:	Yes, on-leash. Waste bins at the trailhead.
AMENITIES:	Street parking, interpretive signs, monument
CONTACT/MAP:	Salt Lake City Public Lands Department
GPS:	40.79174˚N, 111.88816˚W
BEFORE YOU GO:	The 1-mile roundtrip hike to Ensign Peak Monument is very popular. Ensign Peak Preserve hours are 5:00 AM to 10:00 PM. Prime wildflower viewing is in spring and early summer. It's a good cool-weather route.

GETTING THERE

Public Transit: Using public transit adds 1 mile of walking each way. Take UTA bus route 200 to 500 N / Cortez Street and walk east. Turn left on E. Capitol Boulevard and continue for half a mile to Edgecombe Drive. Turn left, and at 0.8 mile, pass Ensign Downs Park where Edgecombe Drive becomes Ensign Vista Drive. At 1 mile, find the trailhead on the left. **Bike Route:** Use the Salt Lake City & County Bikeways Map to plot a route to the trailhead. **Driving:** From I-15, take exit 309 for 600 N and head west for 0.8 mile. Turn right on Wall Street and then left on Zane Avenue. In 0.2 mile, turn right on Columbus Street, followed by an immediate left onto 500 N. Turn left on E. Capitol Boulevard and continue for half a mile. Turn left on Edgecombe Drive, which becomes Ensign Vista Drive after

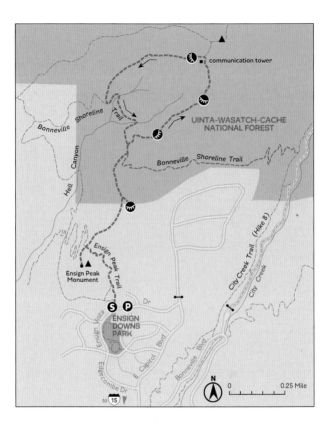

0.3 mile. Reach the Ensign Peak Nature Park and park along the street.

Ensign Peak represents centuries of Utah heritage. The area around Ensign Peak was once a campsite and meeting place for several bands of Shoshoni and Ute Indians. In the late 1700s, nonindigenous mountain men charted mountain passes and explored the area, seeking animal pelts. Two days after the Mormon pioneers arrived in 1847, Brigham Young

Early spring flowers, such as arrowleaf balsamroot, line the trail.

climbed Ensign Peak. Struck by stunning views of the valley and mountains, he declared, "This is the place!"

The 0.5-mile hike to the Ensign Peak Monument gains about 400 feet in elevation. While it's steep, this short trail is understandably well-loved for its history and breathtaking panoramic views. If you're hiking with children or looking for a quick ramble, the monument is a great destination. The remainder of the hike is very steep.

This route as described here visits the monument, then treks the foothills on much quieter trails offering impressive views. During blooming months, the emerald-green hills make a sensational foreground for the dramatic Wasatch peaks. Abundant native wildflowers such as Wasatch bluebells, long-leaf phlox, Utah milkvetch, yellow avalanche-lily (one of the earliest spring wildflowers), and Utah's state flower, the sego lily, are an area highlight.

Aside from a couple of small stands of Gambel oak and bigtooth maple, there is almost no shade. While it's not a good choice for hot days, it's a prime area when temperatures are cooler. If conditions are icy or snowy, the trail past Ensign Peak Monument gets very slick.

GET MOVING

To locate the trailhead, look for the large granite "Ensign Peak Nature Park" sign and follow the sidewalk past a series of interpretive and historical plaques. Within a few hundred feet, the sidewalk becomes the wide, well-worn Ensign Peak Trail. Begin a steep ascent and keep right when the trail forks.

There are a multitude of informal social trails around Ensign Peak Trail and throughout the route; stay on the obvious, well-worn main paths. In spring and summer, the meadows west of the footpath burst into gold as the arrowleaf balsamroot blooms. At 0.4 mile (elevation 5340 feet), the trail comes to a four-way intersection. Go left and climb for 0.1 mile, gaining another 60 feet of elevation to reach the Ensign Peak Monument. Relish an overwhelming view of the Utah State Capitol, downtown, and the Wasatch Mountains, including Grandeur Peak (Hike 15), Mount Olympus (Hike 20), Bells Canyon (Hike 28), and Lone Peak.

Retrace the route back to the four-way intersection, this time going straight, and immediately climb a short, steep hill. Continue scrambling up the rocky trail, and at 0.9 mile (elevation 5610 feet) come to a three-way junction. Take the trail on the right and follow it a short distance until it stops at a sensational overlook. Soak in the views, then retrace your steps back to the three-way intersection. Go straight and enjoy the moderate grade for 0.4 mile.

At 1.2 miles, when the trail forks at the Bonneville Shoreline Trail (BST) go left (right is the Go Farther route). After a few hundred feet, turn right at another fork to begin a 1.7-mile loop. Continue to climb, and at 1.4 miles (elevation 5790 feet),

BONNEVILLE SHORELINE TRAIL

Bonneville Shoreline Trail (BST) is an ambitious trail project that began in 1990. The planned route will one day stretch from the Idaho border to Nephi, south of Provo—nearly 300 miles of trail. The concept includes a pathway along the western slopes of the Wasatch Range and eastern slopes of the Oquirrh Mountains along or close to the shoreline bench of the ancient Lake Bonneville. The proposed project involves building new trail and connecting existing trails in Cache, Box Elder, Weber, Davis, Salt Lake, Utah, and Juab Counties.

Many routes in this guidebook encounter parts of the Bonneville Shoreline Trail. For these encounters, the Bonneville Shoreline Trail is listed. The expansive, changing, and intricate nature of the BST makes it a good candidate for a guidebook of its own. Only a portion of the Salt Lake County section of the BST is touched on in this book. The Bonneville Shoreline Trail Committee is an excellent resource for information, including maps and trail updates.

reach a vista overlooking Memory Grove Park and City Creek Canyon (Hike 8).

Come to another view at 1.7 miles. Continue climbing, and at 1.9 miles come to a junction at a communication tower, which marks the route's high point at 6150 feet elevation. Go left to complete the loop. Look for a small trail sign and a thin dirt trail traversing along the north side of the communication tower fence. Gain the final few feet of elevation, then begin a steep descent. Just past the communication tower, look for a sweeping view of the Oquirrh Mountains and the Great Salt Lake to the west.

Drop more than 500 feet in 0.5 mile before the trail reaches a T intersection at 2.6 miles. Head left on the BST. Enjoy a reprieve from the steep grade and a bit of shade from the stands of mature Gambel oak and bigtooth maple. Complete the loop at 3 miles and encounter the trail you arrived on. For the final mile, retrace your steps back to the trailhead.

GO FARTHER

On the way back, add nearly 700 vertical feet and 2.5 miles of trail on a scenic segment of Bonneville Shoreline Trail. When the trail forks a few feet after completing the loop, go left. Follow the path to descend several switchbacks, then traverse under cliffs.

Around 0.9 mile, the path begins a series of steep switchbacks, descending into City Creek Canyon on a shady lane. At 1.3 miles (elevation 4940 feet), the path intersects City Creek Trail (Hike 8). Find a shady spot for a snack and take a few moments to observe the diverse species thriving around City Creek before heading back. To return, retrace the trail, gain 670 feet of elevation, and then descend the route back to the trailhead.

Note: The Go Farther route traverses avalanche terrain. For winter travel, avalanche education and equipment are recommended.

8 Memory Grove Park and City Creek Canyon

DISTANCE:	9.5-mile loop
ELEVATION GAIN:	1010 feet
HIGH POINT:	5280 feet
DIFFICULTY:	Easy to Moderate
TIME:	Up to 6 hours
FITNESS:	Walkers, hikers, runners
FAMILY-FRIENDLY:	Yes, there are paved pedestrian roadways in both Memory Grove Park and City Creek Canyon, but each has steep sections that may be challenging for strollers or wheelchairs.
DOG-FRIENDLY:	Yes, on-leash in City Creek Canyon for 4.3 miles; out-and-back only. Off-leash in parts of Memory Grove Park; look for signs. Poop bags and waste bins throughout.

AMENITIES:	Parking, restrooms (multiple pit toilets in the canyon are available year-round), drinking water, picnic areas, historical sights, memorials
CONTACT/MAP:	Salt Lake City Public Lands Department; Salt Lake Public Utilities
GPS:	40.77932°N, 111.88635°W
BEFORE YOU GO:	Check with Salt Lake City Public Lands Department (slc.gov/parks) for seasonal hours and regulations. The paved road in City Creek Canyon is open to motor-vehicle traffic on even days from Memorial Day weekend through September 30. City Creek Canyon allows seasonal hunting; for information about dates and restrictions, visit the Utah Division of Wildlife Resources (wildlife.utah.gov/hunting). Trails in City Creek Canyon move through avalanche terrain. For winter travel, avalanche education and equipment are recommended.

GETTING THERE

Public Transit: Take UTA bus route 200 to 500 N / Cortez Street. Walk east on 500 N to E. Capitol Boulevard. The trailhead is just on the other side of E. Capitol Boulevard. **Bike Route:** Use the Salt Lake City & County Bikeways Map to plot a route to the trailhead. **Driving:** From I-15, take exit 309 for 600 N and head east 0.8 mile. Turn right on Wall Street and then go left on Zane Avenue for 0.2 mile. Turn right on Columbus Street, followed by an immediate left on 500 N. Turn right on E. Capitol Boulevard; the capitol's upper parking lot is immediately on the left.

Sometimes, the route itself is the destination. This hike through Memory Grove Park and City Creek Canyon will carry you alongside City Creek, unveiling new discoveries at every turn. The trail along the creek in Memory Grove Park travels under a shady canopy of native box elder, cottonwoods, and western serviceberry. As the course ascends, deciduous forests gradually transform into City Creek Canyon's mature groves of white fir. The preserved open space and limited

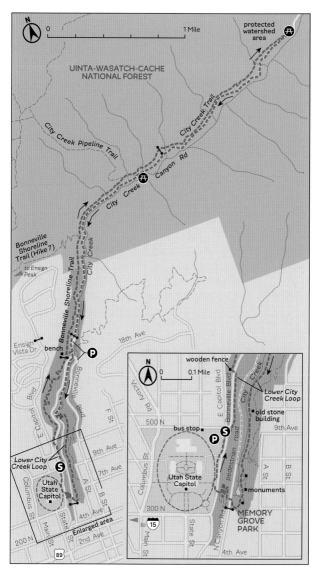

Spring cherry blossoms at the Utah State Capitol, where this hike begins.

human activity allow majestic mountain mammals like cougars, bears, and coyotes to inhabit the area.

The canyon features thirty picnic sites, reservable on even days and holidays during the months that allow vehicle traffic. When the road is closed to vehicle traffic, pedestrians can enjoy picnic areas without a reservation.

Because City Creek Canyon is a watershed, wading or swimming is forbidden. The life-sustaining watercourse provides drinking water for Salt Lake City while supporting a diverse ecology. (Note: The upper part of the canyon does not permit dogs.)

Memory Grove Park and City Creek Canyon feature paved pedestrian walkways. The trail as described here ascends on hiking paths parallel to the pedestrian road, stopping where the single-track hiking trail intersects City Creek Canyon Road. The descent back follows the paved pedestrian paths. For a shorter hike, turn around at any point, or use one of the many exit paths that lead to the pedestrian road. During cold months, micro-traction spikes and poles are recommended.

GET MOVING

From the northeast corner of the Utah State Capitol upper parking lot, use the crosswalk to cross E. Capitol Boulevard. The trail begins at a sign indicating a hiking-only trail named "Lower City Creek Loop." The dirt trail gently traverses the east-facing slope of the canyon, with views of the paved pedestrian lane in Memory Grove Park.

At 0.3 mile, when the trail forks, go left and use the crosswalk to cross Bonneville Boulevard (right goes to Memory Grove Park). Walk through a wooden fence with a hiking-only sign, and begin a gentle ascent through shrubs of greasewood, big sage, lilac, and white sage. The ground cover is abundant in spring and early summer, erupting with wildflowers like yellow avalanche-lily, evening primrose, desert madwort, arrowleaf balsamroot, and cold-desert phlox.

Climb through a few gentle switchbacks around 0.6 mile (elevation 4750 feet), catching supreme views of Wasatch heights like Grandeur Peak (Hike 15), Mount Olympus (Hike 20), and upper Bells Canyon (Hike 28). At 1.1 miles, exit the hiking-only zone through a small gate and come to a well-signed, four-way intersection with a bench. Look for a sign that reads "BST West City Creek" and go left/straight. Right goes to the City Creek Canyon trailhead and parking area (public restrooms).

At 1.5 miles, when the Bonneville Shoreline Trail (BST) merges with a path that leads to City Creek Canyon Road, turn left. The trail mildly ascends and then forks at 1.9 miles; go left. Next veer right at 2.1 miles to enter another foot traffic–only zone; left goes toward Ensign Peak on the BST (Hike 7).

At 2.6 miles, trend left, passing several byways that lead to the visible City Creek Canyon Road. Then at 2.7 miles, where the track merges with City Creek Pipeline Trail, go right. After a few hundred feet, encounter the next fork and turn left. At 3 miles (elevation 5060 feet), pass through a metal gate and then go left. (If the gate is closed due to muddy conditions, turn right and walk a few dozen feet to City Creek Canyon Road, then continue the route on the road.)

For the next 1.25 miles, the footpath runs parallel and often in sight of City Creek Canyon Road. Mature stands of white fir, enormous Gambel oaks, and bigtooth maples give this portion of the canyon a distinct character. The trail forks at 4.3 miles before entering the protected watershed (no dogs allowed). Folks with dogs need to turn around here. The trail continues for another 0.2 mile, reaching the highest point of elevation, 5280 feet, just before it ends at its intersection with City Creek Canyon Road.

To return to the start, descend on the paved pedestrian walkways of City Creek Canyon and Memory Grove Park. The ample picnic areas in City Creek Canyon are an ideal place to stop for snacks and refreshments (take into consideration reservation requirements).

Follow the City Creek Canyon Road for 3.5 miles, and at 8.5 miles from the start, reach the City Creek Canyon gate and trailhead. Use the crosswalk to the other side of Bonneville Boulevard and descend a short gravel path to the paved walkway of Memory Grove Park (off-leash area). Continue for

0.5 mile, then go left over a bridge crossing City Creek. Follow the dirt path and trend right to keep close to the creek. Pass a couple of bridges, then at 9.3 miles, come to the remnants of an old stone building. Pass two more bridges, and at 9.5 miles, when the dirt becomes pavement and forks, go right to explore the Memory Grove Park memorial structures.

Meander through the memorial garden, checking out the plaques and veteran commemorations. When you're ready to head home, locate the Capitol steps and begin the 100-foot ascent. At the top of the stairs, cross the street and go right to return to the parking lot.

GO FARTHER

The Utah State Capitol is a marvelous piece of architecture with splendid marble, stunning art, and fascinating history within. Cherry trees with their infamous spring blossoms line the perimeter of the 0.8-mile gravel pathway that encircles the Capitol. Stop inside, wonder at the architecture, and stroll under the cherry blossoms.

Open Monday through Thursday, 7:00 AM to 8:00 PM, and Friday through Sunday plus holidays, 7:00 AM to 6:00 PM.

9 Red Butte Garden

DISTANCE:	3-mile loop
ELEVATION GAIN:	570 feet
HIGH POINT:	5470 feet
DIFFICULTY:	Easy to Moderate
TIME:	1.5 hours
FITNESS:	Walkers, hikers, runners
FAMILY-FRIENDLY:	Yes, a children's garden and paved trails that are stroller- and ADA-accessible are within the botanical gardens.

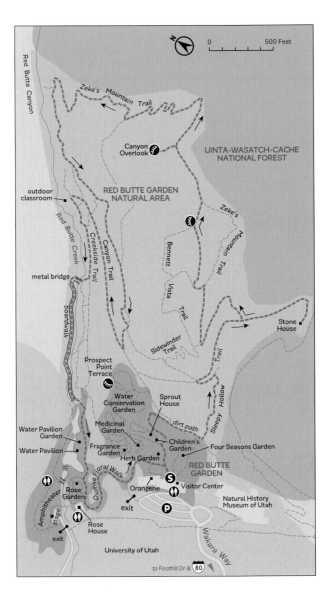

DOG-FRIENDLY:	No, dogs are prohibited.
AMENITIES:	Parking, restrooms, drinking water, interpretive signs, learning centers, picnic areas, benches, maps, gift shop
CONTACT/MAP:	University of Utah / Red Butte Garden
GPS:	40.76525°N, 111.82425°W
BEFORE YOU GO:	Open year-round, Red Butte Garden has an entrance fee, with yearly membership options, discounts for veterans and seniors, and free entry for people who receive food assistance. Some areas are closed during the winter season.

GETTING THERE

Public Transit: Take TRAX Red Line to the University of Utah Medical Station. Cross the street to the bus/shuttle stop. Call 801-581-4189 to arrange transportation through the University of Utah's free on-demand shuttle (pick-up TRAX Medical Station, drop-off Natural History Museum). **Bike Route:** Use the Salt Lake City & County Bikeways Map to plot a route to the trailhead. **Driving:** From I-80, take exit 129 for UT 186 / Foothill Drive and travel north for 3.3 miles. Turn right on Wakara Way and drive 0.8 mile until the road ends at the Red Butte Garden parking area.

Red Butte Garden teems with quiet nooks and sanctuaries for pristine nature bathing, with over 5 miles of private hiking trails that offer a reprieve from noisy crowds. Explore quiet paths filled with pleasant resting places as you follow a wandering loop around the botanical gardens and surrounding natural area.

In 1983, the University of Utah dedicated 100 acres at the mouth of Red Butte Canyon for a regional botanical garden. When it opened to the public in 1985, its mission included conservation and environmental education in addition to horticultural research. Today, Red Butte Garden features one of the largest botanical gardens in the intermountain west.

Highlights within the 21 acres of display gardens include a water conservation garden, 524,000 blooming bulbs in spring,

Extraordinary fall colors line the Reflection Ponds in Red Butte's botanical gardens.

a summer concert series, and locally written poetry displayed throughout the year.

The University of Utah, in conjunction with Red Butte Garden, is the State Arboretum of Utah. Public education, classes, workshops, and events aid Red Butte Garden in pursuing its goal to help the community understand, value, protect, and be enriched by the world of plants.

The main trail described in this hike explores Red Butte Garden's private natural trails, stopping by Stone House, a remnant from the pioneer days, and then passes several noteworthy views of Salt Lake Valley before returning under a canopy of mature trees near Red Butte Creek. Pack a picnic and plan to meander the display gardens after the hike (see Go Farther).

GET MOVING

Enter through the visitor center and gift shop. Take the main paved byway to the left of the courtyard garden. Go right and pass the herb garden, the children's garden, and the sprout house. Turn right onto a wide, double-track dirt path and at 0.2 mile, turn left onto Sleepy Hollow Trail, a narrow footpath.

The trail gently climbs through scrub oak, sage, aspen fleabane, arrowleaf balsamroot, and wild parsley. Go right at the first fork. When the trail forks again at 0.4 mile, go straight to check out Stone House, featuring a superb view of downtown Salt Lake and the Oquirrh Mountains to the west.

When you've finished admiring the view, retrace the trail and this time go right at the fork. At the next junction, go right again, with Red Butte Peak visible to the southeast. The grade steepens and the passage narrows as it climbs next to granite boulders. When you reach a T intersection at 0.9 mile, go left, followed by an immediate right. Climb a ridge and at 1 mile come to an overlook at a fork. Go right and then veer left when the track forks again in a few hundred feet.

At 1.1 miles, the trail reaches its high point (elevation 5470 feet) and forks. Go left and walk a short distance to the Canyon Overlook; peer into Red Butte Canyon and notice the dense trees clustered around Red Butte Creek. When you're ready to continue, retrace your steps and turn left back onto the main passage. Shortly after, the trail takes a hard left and drops elevation on narrow switchbacks. Long after the west- and south-facing regions dry, the trail in this zone holds snow and ice, which turns to mud. During snowy months it's helpful to have micro-traction spikes and poles for this section.

Go right at a fork at 1.4 miles and descend into a mature Gambel oak and bigtooth maple forest. The track veers left, parallel to Red Butte Creek. Encounter a fork at 1.8 miles, go left, and continue trending left, proceeding toward the upper tier of the water conservation garden. At 2 miles, go right, followed by a right onto the Canyon Trail, to head back into the oak and maple forest.

Stay on the Canyon Trail until it comes to a junction at 2.3 miles. Look for the outdoor classroom nestled in a grove of mature trees. Go left on the Creekside Trail and ramble through the forest with Red Butte Creek gurgling to the right. Stay on the most well-worn path to avoid the web of forest byways around the Creekside Trail. At 2.4 miles, look for a metal bridge that crosses over the creek to the right.

Cross the bridge, descend the steps, and mosey down the recently built boardwalk. The boardwalk enters the botanical garden; check out the life-size moose sculpture ahead and then take the left track that skirts around the ponds. Walk past the water pavilion and stay on the main paved trail to pass the rose garden and then a restroom. Then the path enters the Dumke Floral Walk, which is lined with colorful seasonal gardens, passes under a section of stunning pear arbors, and leads to the iconic *Rainbird* statue. To complete the 3-mile loop, follow the floral walk back to the visitor center.

GO FARTHER

No trip to Red Butte Garden is complete without a quiet ramble through the display gardens. Identification plaques and informational signs add depth to the endless variety of flora and fauna: keep an eye out for resident squirrels, porcupines, and birds. A thorough garden loop will add about a mile to the journey.

Picnics and coolers are allowed, with no reservation required for groups of fewer than twenty-five people. Scope out a few ideal picnic locations on your quiet garden saunter, and then grab the cooler and refreshments from the car for a meal immersed in nature.

POETRY IN THE GARDEN

This poem was displayed in Red Butte Garden's "Poetry in the Garden" series from spring 2021 through winter 2022.

Youth Eternal in Spring

I witness spring in awe—
Daffodils shine gold amidst the emerald grasses.
Tulips play peek-a-boo,
then comes iris in indigo blue.
The plum trees glow pink before red leaves grow.
Dogwoods in rose follow.
The apple blossoms white petals—to the sky they wink.
The radiant cobalt kisses green meadows.
Streams a-flow, good-bye snow.
With the new life, I am in wonder.
My heart calls my legs to wander—
into the young mountains to hear the first song
    of the aspen's leaves.
Many search for fountains,
yet I find youth eternal in spring.

    —Ashley Brown

Garden visitors delight in the many spring sights in Red Butte Gardens.

The Red Butte Garden amphitheater is debatably the best venue in Utah. As in the botanical garden, picnics are permitted, but the limited lawn seating is first-come, first-serve. Performing artists and residents alike profess their love for this venue. Tickets typically go on sale from April to May, and most shows sell out.

10 Governors Groves

DISTANCE:	1-mile loop
ELEVATION GAIN:	60 feet
HIGH POINT:	4880 feet
DIFFICULTY:	Easy
TIME:	30 minutes
FITNESS:	Walkers, runners
FAMILY-FRIENDLY:	Yes, the flat gravel paths are jogger stroller–friendly and ADA-accessible with all-terrain wheels.
DOG-FRIENDLY:	Yes, on-leash
AMENITIES:	Interpretive signs, benches
CONTACT/MAP:	This Is The Place Heritage Park
GPS:	40.7532˚N, 111.8214˚W
BEFORE YOU GO:	The parking lot for Scott M. Matheson Preserve is located within the gates of This Is The Place Heritage Park. Preserve admission and parking are free. Open daily from 8:00 AM to 5:00 PM. There isn't much shade in summer, but this is a great choice for a snowy hike.

GETTING THERE

Public Transit: If using public transit, begin the hike on the Go Farther route. Take UTA bus route 3 to This Is The Place Heritage Park. The bus stop is at the entrance of the park. Head west 0.4 mile on the sidewalk to begin. **Bike Route:** Use the Salt Lake City & County Bikeways Map to plot a route to the trailhead. **Driving:** From I-80, take exit 129 for UT 186 W /

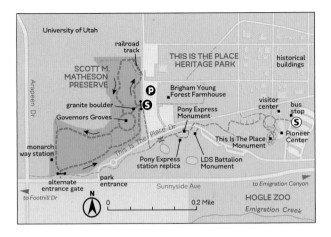

Foothill Drive, and go north on Foothill Drive for 2.9 miles. Turn right on Sunnyside Avenue and head east for 0.4 mile, and then turn left into This Is The Place Heritage Park. Drive for 0.2 mile and turn left to enter the parking lot.

The Scott M. Matheson Nature Preserve and Governors Groves lie at the entrance to This Is The Place Heritage Park. Dedicated in 2004, the 14-acre preserve connects users to Utah's historical roots while simultaneously protecting its native habitat. The vegetation here mimics the type of flora Mormon pioneers saw when they first arrived in Utah in 1847—the space is rich with ground cover and scattered trees, including chokecherry, cottonwood, pinyon pine, big sagebrush, hawthorn, Woods' rose, and rabbitbrush.

Governors Groves is at the heart of the preserve; here you'll find a granite marker and information about each of the seventeen Utah state governors, including Scott M. Matheson, for whom the preserve is named. The paths are wide, gravel, and relatively flat. Circle the preserve and then explore Governors Groves after strolling the grounds.

GET MOVING

The preserve entrance is on the west side of the parking area; enter through a metal gate. Once through the gate, find a three-way junction and a large granite boulder commemorating the preserve to the left. Go right and then immediately veer right again, strolling along the eastern boundary.

After a few hundred feet, the trail diverges. Go right, and in a few moments, reach a three-way fork. Take the middle branch and walk across a section of narrow-gauge railroad tracks. Reconstructed in 2002, this segment of railroad uses vintage rails from the 1800s on the original railbed; check out the interpretive sign below the tracks. At the end of the tracks, take a left to reconnect with the main trail, at just over 0.1 mile.

Go straight for a few hundred feet until the trail forks. Some benches and wooden seats are visible on a grassy hill straight ahead; if a rest beckons, meander up the grass slope. If not, go left for 0.1 mile to reach another junction, which marks 0.3 mile from the start.

Go right, and after a few steps, take another right to begin curving around the perimeter of Governors Groves. Turn right again to gain a track heading west. Saunter through fields of alfalfa, blue wildrye, bitter dock, and sage. The trail curves left 0.5 mile from the starting point, and in a few hundred feet, reach a monarch butterfly way station, which provides milkweed, nectar, and shelter essential for monarch migration.

Past the butterfly station, an alternate entrance gate leads to Sunnyside Avenue on the right. Pass by the gate and head back toward the parking area. At the next two junctions, stay right to return to the original entrance gate, and then turn left to visit Governors Groves. Read all about the history of Utah's governors on the 0.1-mile loop before exiting the preserve.

Opposite: *Sunflowers line the sidewalks of This Is The Place Heritage Park.*

GO FARTHER

For an interesting cultural experience, take a 0.9-mile tour of the statues in This Is The Place Heritage Park, an ode to Utah's Mormon pioneer history.

Start by investigating the Brigham Young Forest Farmhouse, a large pink structure across the parking lot from the Scott M. Matheson Preserve. After you've checked out the farmhouse, head back toward the preserve parking lot entrance, cross the street (with caution), and go left on the sidewalk to cross a bridge. Head up the walkway for a few hundred feet and turn right to loop around a replica of a Pony Express station. Return to the sidewalk and continue to a second tribute to the Pony Express, a monument named *Changing Horses*, followed by The Church of Jesus Christ of Latter-day Saints Battalion Monument.

Cross the street to follow the trail past several more Church of Jesus Christ of Latter-day Saints heritage statues on the left, with views of This Is The Place Monument ahead. The walkway leads to the visitor center (public transportation start), 0.4 mile from the Scott M. Matheson Preserve parking area. Plan your visit during operating hours to visit the café, gift shop, or the pioneer village (paid entry). Head back on the same route.

11 Miller Bird Refuge and Bonneville Glen

DISTANCE:	1-mile loop
ELEVATION GAIN:	110 feet
HIGH POINT:	4650 feet
DIFFICULTY:	Easy
TIME:	30 minutes
FITNESS:	Walkers, runners

FAMILY-FRIENDLY: Yes

DOG-FRIENDLY: On-leash in Miller Bird Refuge; poop bags and waste bins at the north and west park entrances. Dogs are not allowed in Bonneville Glen.

AMENITIES: Interpretive signs, parking, benches

CONTACT/MAP: Salt Lake City Public Lands Department

GPS: 40.74974°N, 111.84177°W

BEFORE YOU GO: Miller Bird Refuge and Nature Park is open from 5:00 AM to 9:00 PM. Bonneville Glen, open from 5:00 AM to 10:00 PM, is privately owned and maintained by the LDS Salt Lake Bonneville Stake.

GETTING THERE

Public Transit: Take UTA bus route 9 to 900 S / 1500 E (east-bound buses) or Greenwood Terrace / 900 S (southbound buses). Go east on 900 S for about a quarter mile. The north entrance to Miller Bird Refuge and Nature Park is on the right. **Bike Route:** Use the Salt Lake City & County Bikeways Map to plot a route to the trailhead. **Driving:** From Foothill Drive,

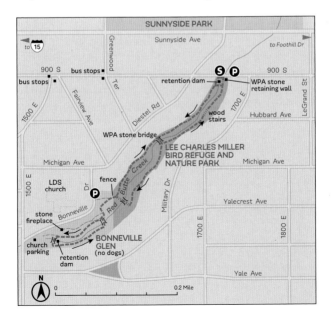

go west on Sunnyside Avenue for 0.4 mile. Turn left on Le Grand Street and then take the next right on 900 S. The north entrance to Miller Bird Refuge and Nature Park is on the left in 0.2 mile. Park on 900 S.

> *This park isn't just a refuge for birds. It's a refuge for students of all ages—for anyone curious about the amazing community of plants and animals that make this place home.*
>
> —MILLER BIRD REFUGE AND NATURE PARK WELCOME SIGN

The Lee Charles Miller Bird Refuge and Nature Park is a slice of wilderness heaven nestled within the surrounding urban hustle. Minnie Miller donated the land to create the park in honor of her last husband in 1935, envisioning a sanctuary for both wildlife and children. Nearly a century after Minnie's gift, this 9-acre park continues to offer a much-needed reprieve from the bustling city life.

The trickle of running water, a graceful canopy of native trees, and the songs of various birds like the downy woodpecker, ruby-crowned kinglet, and black-chinned hummingbirds soothe the soul. Stunning masonry structures add depth and beauty to the walking paths. The historical masonry work was completed during the Great Depression by the Works Progress Administration (WPA) and remains in excellent condition today.

Follow this short walk as it encircles Red Butte Creek and hugs the property of private residents on a gentle, all-season dirt trail. When the trail is snow-covered, micro-traction spikes and hiking poles are recommended.

GET MOVING

A fence and several signs mark the preserve's entrance on 900 S. The historical stone steps diverge before descending into the sanctuary. Go left and walk into a canopy of native

Maple leaves are golden confetti on this nearly century-old stone bridge.

trees like box elder, cottonwood, red-osier dogwood, choke-cherry, and Rocky Mountain maple, enjoying the ample shade and sound absorption they provide.

At the base of the stairs, reach a WPA stone retaining wall, a park map, and an interpretive sign. Turn right on the sheltered dirt path to begin the loop.

Meander on the gentle walkway with Red Butte Creek running parallel on your left. Reach a WPA-crafted stone bridge 0.2 mile from the park entrance; turn left to cross over the bridge. Then go right and ascend a brief steep section. In another 0.1 mile, the path leads to a short flight of stairs and a second bridge. Cross the bridge to climb another staircase. At the top, go left and walk for a few moments to reach a fence and the west entrance of Miller Bird Refuge.

Exit the bird refuge through the fence to explore Bonneville Glen (dogs not permitted). Immediately go left at the fork (right leads to street parking on Bonneview Drive). Descend for several hundred feet to a junction—veer right and avoid crossing the bridge. Go left at the next fork to stay on the main path, with Red Butte Creek gurgling to the left.

At 0.4 mile, the trail reaches an astounding outdoor fireplace and stone structure, where the trail forks. Go left and cross Red Butte Creek at a retention dam. Follow the way with Red Butte Creek now on your left.

The trail crosses a bridge at 0.6 mile and comes to an intersection. Go right and retrace the route back to Miller Bird Refuge, entering through the same fence you used to exit. Then go straight, passing the stairs on the right.

Stroll along the inviting path for 0.1 mile to reach the WPA stone bridge for the second time. Cross the bridge again and go left to complete the final quarter mile. The trail wanders close to Red Butte Creek, offering an opportunity to look for native fish species like Bonneville cutthroat trout and June sucker.

Reach wood stairs at just over 0.8 mile from the start. Ascend the stairs and continue toward the park entrance. Before leaving the sanctuary, go left and cross a retention dam to read a commemorative plaque and take in views of Red Butte Creek. To exit the park, walk to the opposite side of the retention dam. Take a left and then an almost immediate sharp right to ascend the stone stairs to 900 S.

GO FARTHER

For more mileage, walk the loop two or three times. Are you interested in practicing stewardship? Check out the city's Adopt-A-Spot program, where volunteers pull weeds, plant native vegetation, monitor wildlife, collect trash, and more. To get involved, call 801-972-7800.

12 Liberty Park

DISTANCE:	1.5-mile loop plus 3 miles of trails
ELEVATION GAIN:	20 feet
HIGH POINT:	4270 feet
DIFFICULTY:	Easy
TIME:	45 minutes
FITNESS:	Walkers, runners
FAMILY-FRIENDLY:	Yes, the flat, paved loop is ADA-accessible and perfect for strollers.
DOG-FRIENDLY:	Yes, on-leash. Waste bins throughout.
AMENITIES:	Parking, restrooms, drinking water, fishing pond, playgrounds, picnic tables, BBQ grills, pavilion, volleyball court, basketball court, bocce ball, horseshoes, historical sites, Chase Home Museum of Utah Folk Arts, seasonal farmers' market. Paid entrance to swimming pool, tennis courts, paddle boats, carnival rides, aviary.
CONTACT/MAP:	Salt Lake City Public Lands Department
GPS:	40.74431°N, 111.87566°W
BEFORE YOU GO:	A popular year-round destination. Playground hours are 7:00 AM to 11:00 PM. Mature trees make Liberty Park an excellent choice for hot days.

GETTING THERE

Public Transit: Take UTA bus route 205 to 500 E / 1111 S (northbound buses) or 500 E / 1104 S (southbound buses). The bus stop is across the street from Liberty Park. Walk east to cross 500 S and enter Liberty Park. **Bike Route:** Use the Salt Lake City & County Bikeways Map to plot a route to the trailhead. **Driving:** From I-80, take exit 125 for UT 71 / 700 E, and go north on 700 E for 2.9 miles. Turn left on 900 S, and then take the next left to enter Constitution Drive, the one-way road encircling Liberty Park. There are parking spots surrounding the park. The trail starts from the largest parking lot, near the public pool and Tracy Aviary.

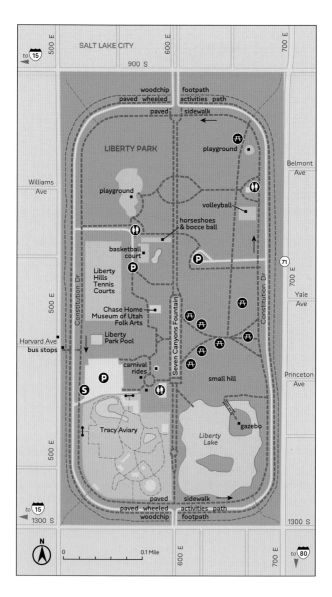

A visit to Liberty Park is an opportunity to hear diverse languages, see and smell gourmet ethnic picnic cuisines, and witness the variety of cultures that make up Salt Lake City. From family potlucks to romantic picnics to solitary meditations, almost any conceivable park-related activity has a place here.

Liberty Park has been serving Salt Lake residents as a restful sanctuary for over 140 years. In the mid-1800s, the property was a grist mill and farm. When Brigham Young acquired ownership of the 110-acre farm in 1860, he planted mulberry and cottonwood trees, many of which still stand today. Salt Lake City Corporation purchased the land in 1880, and by the 1920s, the park boasted playgrounds, tennis courts, lakes, and many other amenities.

As the oldest city park in Salt Lake, the most-prized feature of Liberty Park is its robust groves of trees with their massive canopies. The sprawling tree cover offers pleasant, shady spots on hot summer days.

Three circular 1.5-mile pedestrian walkways encircle the park: the path on the inside perimeter of Constitution Drive is a sidewalk; the middle path on the outside perimeter of Constitution Drive is for wheeled activities, including strollers, bikes, skates, and wheelchairs; and the outermost circle is a woodchip footpath for walkers and runners only.

GET MOVING

Begin from the parking area near the Tracy Aviary entrance and head west toward the paths around the park's perimeter. Choose the woodchip path for walking and jogging or the pedestrian road for strollers or wheelchairs. Go south to begin the 1.5-mile counterclockwise loop.

For the first 0.25 mile, watch for glimpses of exotic birds and raptors in Tracy Aviary's botanical gardens (see Go Farther). On the park's southern border, enormous box elders and ponderosa pines line the path. The next quarter mile borders

People from all walks of life meander Liberty Park under the shade of mature trees.

Liberty Lake, a pretty water feature teeming with birdlife (seasonal paddle boat rentals available).

On the park's eastern edge, gigantic Fremont cottonwoods, English oak, and horse chestnut trees shade the lane. At 1 mile, pass the 900 S entrance and then a large playground as the trail turns south. Look for the public Liberty Hills Tennis Center on the left (open seven days a week; fee required). Next to the tennis center is the outdoor Liberty Park Pool. Maintained by Salt Lake County, the pool operates seasonally, with an entrance fee. After the pool, come to the Tracy Aviary parking lot, which marks the completion of the 1.5-mile loop.

Don't leave after the first loop—plan for time to wander the park's interior. Visit the Chase Home Museum of Utah Folk Arts on Thursday, Friday, or Saturday from 10:00 AM to 4:00 PM to enjoy a complimentary tour of more than 450 pieces of art, featuring displays from the European, Asian, Latinx, Pacific Islander, and African communities of Utah.

Walk the Seven Canyons Fountain, a public art structure emulating the Wasatch Front mountains and the seven major watercourses that flow into the Jordan River. Although the city intentionally turned off the fountain's water in 2017 for conservation and sanitization reasons, it continues to serve as an aesthetic and educational structure.

Meander around Liberty Lake and cross the footbridge to a gazebo, a perfect spot for a picnic or some bird-watching. To top off your Liberty Park exploration, climb the small hill north of Liberty Lake for a stunning view of Mount Olympus (Hike 20).

GO FARTHER

Tracy Aviary is one of the oldest free-standing aviaries in the United States. The impressive bird and plant species collection makes the entry fee a worthwhile educational investment. A few highlights include aviculture talks, a pelican pond, the owl forest, an indoor rainforest, a café, and a gift shop. Open year-round, 9:00 AM to 5:00 PM. Check the website for admission fees (discounts available).

13 Wasatch Hollow Preserve

DISTANCE:	1-mile loop
ELEVATION GAIN:	60 feet
HIGH POINT:	4560 feet
DIFFICULTY:	Easy
TIME:	30 minutes
FITNESS:	Walkers, hikers, runners
FAMILY-FRIENDLY:	Yes
DOG-FRIENDLY:	Yes, with restrictions. Dogs are not permitted in the north area of the preserve and must be on-leash to walk the south loop. The open field outside the preserve is an off-leash zone from 5:00 AM to 10:00 AM and 5:00 PM to 10:00 PM.
AMENITIES:	Restrooms, pavilion, picnic table, benches, play area, interpretive signs
CONTACT/MAP:	Salt Lake County Parks and Open Space
GPS:	40.73378°N, 111.84410°W
BEFORE YOU GO:	Preserve hours are 5:00 AM to 11:00 PM.

GETTING THERE

Public Transit: Take UTA bus route 17 and get off on 1700 S / 1488 E. Locate the 1700 S / 1500 E intersection and head east to cross 1500 E. Walk east on 1700 S for 0.2 mile to reach the Wasatch Hollow Preserve parking area on the left. **Bike Route:** Use the Salt Lake City & County Bikeways Map to plot a route to the trailhead. **Driving:** From I-80, take exit 126 for 1300 E and head north for 1 mile. Turn right on 1700 S, continue for 0.5 mile, and then look for the Wasatch Hollow Preserve parking on the left. If you reach 1700 E, you've passed the preserve.

In Wasatch Hollow Preserve, flowering plants and vines cover the ground and light up the landscape with color from late spring through autumn. A towering canopy of mature cottonwoods, box elder, and peachleaf willow provides shade for

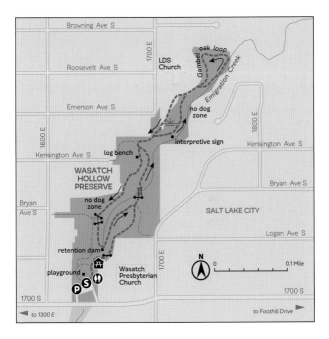

most of the hike. The understory and shrub layers include coyote willow, dogwood, Woods' rose, and scrub oak.

All this beautiful flora was on the brink of destruction when the area was slated for development, until a group of local residents got involved. They teamed up with city and county open space organizations and Utah Open Lands, and in 2009, their combined efforts created the 11-acre Wasatch Hollow Preserve, a permanently protected open space.

Emigration Creek runs through the preserve and provides a critical space for native species. One of Wasatch Hollow's missions is to restore a healthy streamside or riparian habitat. The reestablished riparian environment includes wetlands fed by high water levels, and in turn, the wetlands support animal life.

Despite being surrounded by development, wildlife activity is surprisingly busy. As you amble through the preserve on a

Restored riparian habitat thrives with plant life diversity.

winding figure-eight loop, listen and watch for mule deer, Bonneville cutthroat trout, red-tailed hawks, kestrels, nighthawks, and song sparrows.

GET MOVING

From the parking area, follow the sidewalk to a pavilion and picnic table and then head northeast toward the preserve gate. Enter the gate 250 feet from the parking area.

Once in the preserve, stroll down a gravel path. Look for common sunflowers, showy goldeneyes, and white sage. Arrive at an intersection, go straight onto a wider path, and locate the bridge with the north loop access gate. Open the gate into the "no dog zone" and cross the bridge under a canopy of mature trees. Turn right after the bridge and walk for 250 feet to reach a place where two trails converge, 0.2 mile from the parking area. Proceed straight and come to a T intersection; turn right to avoid exiting the preserve into a neighborhood.

Continue to veer right on the path as it runs parallel to the fence around the preserve. Look for a break in the fence and an interpretive sign to the right. To the left is a wetland teeming with ground cover and shrubs, like giant sage, creeping bellflower, spider flower, and goldenrod.

The trail forks at 0.4 mile; head right to begin a 0.1-mile counterclockwise loop under large Gambel oaks. Stay on the main path to avoid wandering onto private property. The high point of the hike (elevation 4560 feet) is midway through the Gambel oak loop.

Emerge from the loop and go right. At the next junction, veer right again. Continue to trend right until you reach a log bench, an excellent place to stop and soak in some nurturing nature sounds.

Once you've finished drinking in the natural beauty, continue on the trail. In fall, keep an eye out for vibrant gold rabbitbrush. At 0.8 mile, reach another gate that opens to the off-leash dog zone. Exit the gate. Directly across from it, enter the gate for the south loop (on-leash dog area).

Emigration Creek goes underground after a few hundred feet—you'll see a retention dam on the right. From here, locate the entrance path, go right to exit the preserve, and retrace your steps to the parking area.

GO FURTHER

The interpretive signs are brimming with stimulating information about the area. Give yourself extra time to read the signs, then find a quiet viewing place. See how many native plants and animals you can spot.

Next page: *Golden aspens reflected on Lake Desolation in early fall. (Hike 17)*

MILL CREEK CANYON

Mill Creek Canyon is less than a mile from I-215, yet the steep canyon walls and soaring peaks provide immediate relief from the zooming pace of civilization. The deep chasm crowned with ridges and summits combines with a rich riparian ecosystem to fill the area with treasures.

Extended acres of natural space make Mill Creek Canyon an ideal home for regal mountain animals like cougars, elk, moose, and deer. The arid south-facing slopes are adorned with big sage, curl-leaf mountain mahogany, and other heat-loving specimens. The north-facing slopes feature rich coniferous forests. As Mill Creek Canyon Road ascends, the canyon walls narrow and the road enters a dense tunnel of aspen, maple, and spruce. The end of the canyon road is 3000 feet higher than the Salt Lake City center and is significantly cooler.

Hikes in the area offer diverse experiences, from rigorous mountain climbs to gentle forests walks. Ample recreational opportunities and dog-friendly policies make Mill Creek Canyon a popular year-round destination, especially on the weekends. All trails are open to hikers, while mountain bikers and equestrians are allowed only on specific routes. On-leash dogs are allowed on all trails and can be off-leash on odd-numbered days. (Please note that Mill Creek Canyon borders wilderness and watershed areas that are closed to dogs.)

Unlike most hikes in the book, there is a fee to enter Mill Creek Canyon, payable upon exiting; day and annual passes are available. There is no public transportation or cell phone service.

The winter gate closes to vehicle traffic on November 1 and reopens in the summer. In the winter, the closed road beyond the winter gate is a backcountry skiing, cross-country skiing, and snow-shoeing destination.

14 Pipeline Trail

DISTANCE:	9 miles one way
ELEVATION GAIN:	20 to 1550 feet
HIGH POINT:	6640 feet
DIFFICULTY:	Easy to moderate
TIME:	1 to 6 hours
FITNESS:	Hikers, runners
FAMILY-FRIENDLY:	Yes
DOG-FRIENDLY:	Yes, but note that dogs need to be on-leash on even-numbered days. Poop bags and waste bins at the trailheads.
AMENITIES:	Parking, restrooms, trail map, trail signs, and picnic tables (Church Fork)
CONTACT/MAP:	US Forest Service
GPS:	40.69151˚N, 111.76898˚W
BEFORE YOU GO:	Fee area. Mountain bikes are always permitted on the Pipeline Trail. Open to equestrians. Common rattlesnake sightings. Seasonal road closure. No cell phone service. For winter travel, avalanche education and equipment are recommended.

GETTING THERE

Driving: From I-215, take exit 4 and go east on 3900 S for 0.2 mile. Turn left on Wasatch Boulevard. Turn right on 3800 S / Mill Creek Canyon Road and drive for 0.7 mile to reach the tollbooth (pay when exiting). Travel another 0.7 mile to the Rattlesnake Gulch trailhead and parking on the left. There are three other access trailheads for Pipeline Trail: Church Fork, 2.3 miles past the tollbooth (Hike 15); Burch Hollow, 3.6 miles past the tollbooth; and Elbow Fork (Hike 16), 5.4 miles past the tollbooth. The winter road closure is at Maple Grove picnic area, 3.9 miles past the tollbooth.

The Pipeline Trail follows a portion of the old pipeline tread once used to carry copious quantities of water for power

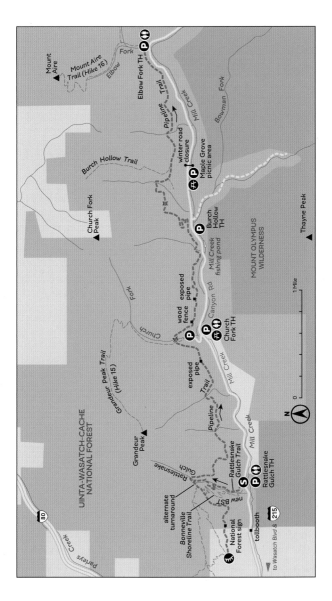

generation. The power station and pipeline were abandoned after years of use, but today you can still see occasional pieces of gigantic pipe along the trail. This trail is now one of Mill Creek's most heavily trafficked routes, and with good reason. The multiple trailheads make it easy to use it for a rigorous workout or a gentle stroll. Because it's mostly dirt and a mellow grade, Pipeline is a favorite for trail runners.

The stretch of Pipeline Trail between the overlook (accessed via Rattlesnake Gulch) and Church Fork is almost entirely flat and has very little shade, which makes it a popular cool-weather choice. During the summer, bring ample water. The steepest sections are between Burch Hollow and Elbow Fork and the access trail from Rattlesnake Gulch. Because it's a west-facing route, it's one of the earliest trails to dry out in the spring; however, be prepared to encounter mud as the snow melts. During the winter, hiking poles and micro-traction spikes are recommended.

The 9-mile, 1550-foot-elevation-gain hike described here starts at the Rattlesnake Gulch trailhead, goes west to the overlook, and then travels up the canyon to the Elbow Fork trailhead. The mileage is one-way; take a car or bike shuttle to get from Elbow Fork back to the Rattlesnake Gulch trailhead. Or use the description to mix and match segments and design an outing to suit your day.

GET MOVING

Locate the pit toilets at the southern end of the parking lot, pass an information kiosk, and begin your hike on a wide, rocky trail that narrows after a few hundred feet.

The Rattlesnake Gulch trailhead is the lowest recreation access point in the canyon (elevation 5330 feet) and the climb up is steep, gaining more than 600 feet in the first 0.8 mile. The trail ascends under a tunnel of Gambel oak and bigtooth maples, which offer welcome shade on hot days and paint the scene with warm hues in autumn. Chokecherries,

The Pipeline Trail offers sweeping vistas over the valley.

Woods' rose, shrubby cinquefoil, and nettleleaf horsemint punctuate the tunnel of green with vibrant colors in spring and early summer.

Look for a large boulder at a directional sign at 0.4 mile and follow the arrow to go left, beginning a series of switchbacks. Reach a signed T intersection at 0.8 mile (elevation 5950 feet): left goes 1 mile to the overlook; right goes 2 miles to Church Fork.

Go left and hike the exposed trail to the overlook. After several paces, the path merges with the Pipeline Trail. Then in a few hundred feet, veer left to remain on the Pipeline Trail. At 1 mile, the newly constructed Bonneville Shoreline Trail (under new development) appears to the left. Stay right and at 1.5 miles encounter a sign that reads "Leaving Wasatch National Forest." To the south stands the immense face and peak of iconic Mount Olympus (Hike 20), with a clear view of *The West Slabs* alpine climbing route.

Pass a cluster of junipers before arriving at the lookout 1.8 miles from the start (elevation 5970 feet). Gaze west to Kennecott Copper Mine and the peaks of the Oquirrh Mountains towering above Blackridge (Hike 42) and Oquirrh Lake Loop (Hike 41). The expanse of Salt Lake Valley lies below.

After admiring the scene, follow the trail back toward Rattlesnake Gulch. At 2.8 miles, you will arrive again at the signed junction at the top of Rattlesnake Gulch Trail. Here you have a choice: If you've had your fill of nature bathing for the day, head right and retrace your steps to the Rattlesnake Gulch parking area to complete your 3.6-mile roundtrip adventure. If you're craving more wilderness time, veer left toward the Church Fork/Grandeur Peak Trail. After a few feet, Rattlesnake Gulch Trails merges with the Pipeline Trail. The path gains less than 20 feet of elevation over the next 2 miles as it meanders among big sage, fleabane, and goldenrod.

The first substantial shady section of the Pipeline Trail begins 1.4 miles after the Rattlesnake Gulch intersection. Travel another 0.2 mile, and look for a large piece of exposed pipe.

Approaching Church Fork, the stream is audible before it's visible. The vegetation changes dramatically as box elders, white firs, Pacific ninebark, and wild hollyhocks crowd the trail, making Church Fork a perfect spot for a shady break by the creek.

At 5 miles from the start (elevation 5990 feet), encounter a signed four-way junction: left goes north to Grandeur Peak (Hike 15), right goes south 0.1 mile to the Church Fork trailhead, and straight crosses a small wooden footbridge to continue east on Pipeline.

Cross the bridge and proceed 0.2 mile past Church Fork to a large wood fence preventing trail erosion. Go another 0.3 mile to another piece of exposed pipe, where the oaks and maples grow tall enough to shade the route for the next quarter of a mile. Keep walking and look for the Mill Creek fishing pond, visible in the canyon below.

Encounter a fork 6.3 miles from the start (elevation 6020 feet) and go left to stay on the Pipeline Trail. (To the right is the 0.2-mile path accessing the Burch Hollow trailhead.) Immediately begin climbing; the trail gains more than 600 feet of elevation in the next 1.5 miles.

A series of switchbacks zigzag up the slope for half a mile, and then a view of Thayne Peak and Gobblers Knob opens to the south. Cross a tiny wooden bridge. After the bridge, the shade increases along with the biodiversity—asters, Oregon grape, and showy goldeneyes pop like confetti among the cutgrass and curl-leaf mountain mahogany.

Reach a three-way junction 7.6 miles from the start (elevation 6600 feet) and go left. After several minutes of walking, meet the signed Burch Hollow Trail to the left; go straight to stay on the Pipeline Trail. Over the next 1.4 miles, enjoy a primarily flat ramble, crossing a couple of drainages and weaving in and out of dense forest.

Your 9-mile, one-way excursion ends at the hike's highest elevation point—6640 feet—by the Elbow Fork/Mount Aire trailhead. Take a car or bike shuttle back to Rattlesnake Gulch trailhead.

15 Grandeur Peak

DISTANCE:	6 miles
ELEVATION GAIN:	2420 feet
HIGH POINT:	8220 feet
DIFFICULTY:	Challenging
TIME:	4 hours
FITNESS:	Hikers, runners
FAMILY-FRIENDLY:	The trail is steep and challenging.
DOG-FRIENDLY:	Yes, but note that dogs need to be on-leash on even-numbered days. Poop bags and waste bins at the trailhead.
AMENITIES:	Parking, restrooms (June 1 to September 30), picnic sites (reservations required), drinking water, trail signs
CONTACT/MAP:	US Forest Service
GPS:	40.70064°N, 111.74250°W
BEFORE YOU GO:	Fee area. The trail is open to equestrians. Prime wildflower months are June through August. No cell phone service. For winter travel, avalanche education and equipment are recommended. Seasonal road closure (Church Fork picnic area access road is closed October 1 to May 31).

GETTING THERE

Driving: From I-215, take exit 4 and go east for 0.2 mile on 3900 S. Turn left on Wasatch Boulevard and then right on 3800 S / Mill Creek Canyon Road. After 0.7 mile, reach the tollbooth (pay when exiting). Continue for 2.3 miles, then look for the Church Fork picnic area on the left. Park on the road or turn left into the picnic area and follow the road for 0.3 mile to the trailhead. Note: This is a heavily used trailhead with just eight parking spots; parking at the Church Fork picnic sites is strictly for picnickers.

Grandeur Peak is an immensely rewarding climb, with stellar views, extraordinary wildflowers in late spring and early summer, and lots of company. The path treks through an emerald

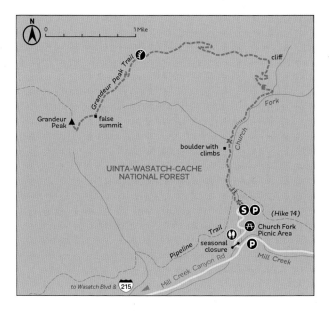

tunnel of ground cover and a canopy of mature trees as it climbs next to the gurgling Church Fork stream.

Understandably, Grandeur Peak attracts all kinds of recreationists, from wilderness novices to seasoned hikers. Grandeur is also a training ground for ultra-marathon athletes; some runners will sweat through two or three laps in a single day.

The upper portion of Grandeur is exposed and can be very hot. The temperature increases drastically about a mile in as the footpath moves away from the dense vegetation surrounding the creek and begins climbing up the southerly slopes. Bring ample water. During snowy months, micro-traction spikes and poles are recommended.

GET MOVING

If you parked on Mill Creek Canyon Road, locate the entrance to the Church Fork picnic area. Be cautious of vehicle traffic

A hiker approaches the false summit of Grander Peak.

as you walk the 0.3 mile to the end of the road, where you'll find the trailhead (Note: Mileage and elevation gain measurements for this hike begin at the trailhead.)

At the trailhead (elevation 5870 feet), locate a well-worn dirt path leading to a trail sign and map. After a couple of hundred feet, cross a cascading stream on a small wooden bridge. Come to a signed intersection with the Pipeline Trail (Hike 16) at 0.1 mile and go straight.

Over the next mile, the passage ascends under massive white firs, box elders, maples, and western serviceberry trees. The steep, well-worn path is a whirl of color during the blooming months; watch for spreading dogbane bushes with tiny, bell-shaped pink flowers. At 0.4 mile, keep an eye out for a large boulder with several climbing routes to the left. Cross a second wood bridge at 0.5 mile and then ascend a steep set of wood-supported stairs.

After climbing over 700 feet, about 1 mile from the trailhead, a sign indicates that the trail turns left from the creek. Move away from the watercourse to begin switchbacks. Mature trees give way to Gambel oaks, scattered big sage, and a rainbow of wildflowers. The colorful display during the summer is a perfect distraction from the steep climb. Lewis flax, Whipple's penstemon, silky lupine, sticky purple geranium, wild hollyhock, and aspen fleabane flash showy shades of purple. Fields of arrowleaf balsamroot gleam golden, and the intricate white, magenta, and yellow petals of Utah's state flower, the sego lily, warrant a pause of appreciation.

Continue up as the trail alternates between full-sun exposure and dappled shade. Around 1.8 miles, the trail gets much rockier. A large cliff (elevation 7280 feet) offers an excellent spot for a breather, with views of Mount Raymond, Wildcat Ridge, and Triangle Peak to the south. The trail turns from the cliff to another inspiring sight: Grandeur Peak, your end goal. It's a powerful motivator to keep on for the final mile (1000 feet of elevation gain).

This part of the hike is the most challenging, with more exposure and obstacles, including several large boulders. At 2.3 miles and 7610 feet elevation, a small alcove to the right offers the first views of Salt Lake Valley. Continue up a steep incline for another half mile and reach the false summit at 2.8 miles. After the false summit, follow the saddle and begin the final climb to Grandeur Peak. Several trails wind up the slope; stick to the most well-worn path.

Reach the summit 3 miles from the start (elevation 8220 feet). Your reward for the challenging climb is a breathtaking bird's-eye view. Directly south and across Mill Creek drainage, look for Mount Olympus (Hike 20), with its alpine climbing routes, *The West Slabs* and *Kamp's Ridge*, in view. The Oquirrh Mountains rise to the west—see if you can spot Blackridge

(Hike 42), which lies south of the easily distinguished Kennecott Copper Mine. The Great Salt Lake and Antelope Island lie to the northwest; Parleys Canyon and the Mountain Dell Reservoir to the northeast. Savor the sights before retracing the 3 miles back to the trailhead.

GO FARTHER
Make a day of it by tackling the Grandeur hike and then retreat to the Church Fork picnic area for rest and replenishment. An ideal retreat to beat the summer heat, a dozen well-shaded picnic spots are scattered around the Church Fork stream. There are even a couple of small waterfalls in the picnicking zone. Call 801-483-5473 to make a seasonal reservation from June 1 to September 30. The picnic area closes at 10:00 PM.

16 Mount Aire

DISTANCE:	3.8 miles
ELEVATION GAIN:	1970 feet
HIGH POINT:	8610 feet
DIFFICULTY:	Challenging
TIME:	3 hours
FITNESS:	Hikers
FAMILY-FRIENDLY:	The trail is steep and challenging.
DOG-FRIENDLY:	Yes, but note that dogs need to be on-leash on even-numbered days. Poop bags and waste bin at the trailhead.
AMENITIES:	Parking, pit toilets
CONTACT/MAP:	US Forest Service
GPS:	40.70692˚N, 111.68988˚W
BEFORE YOU GO:	Fee area. Trail open to equestrians. Occasional rattlesnake sightings. Prime wildflower months are June to early August. Seasonal road closure. No cell phone service. For winter travel, avalanche education and equipment are recommended.

GETTING THERE

Driving: From I-215, take exit 4 and go east 0.2 mile on 3900 S. Turn left on Wasatch Boulevard and then right on 3800 S / Mill Creek Canyon Road. Drive for 0.7 mile to reach the toll-booth (pay when exiting) and then continue 5.4 miles to the Elbow Fork trailhead. There is a small parking lot on the left next to a restroom, and another small lot across Mill Creek Canyon Road. The winter road closure at Maple Grove picnic area adds 1.5 miles of walking each way.

Reaching the summit of Mount Aire is undeniably rewarding, with a 360-degree view of the Wasatch Mountains from a unique perspective. The first half of the trail weaves up steep hills blanketed with wildflowers beneath a canopy of immense firs and quaking aspen stands. The stunning flora, gurgling creek, and birdsong create a soothing sensory experience.

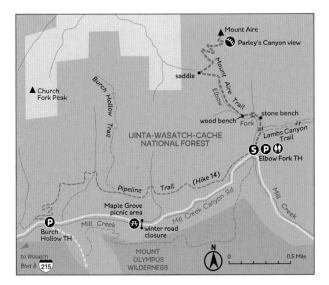

The second part of the hike climbs away from the creek and into a different ecosystem as it ascends Mount Aire's shrubby slopes.

The dirt trail is well-defined and mostly hard-packed, making the extremely steep trail feel approachable. With several stops along the way, the canyon is an inviting endeavor even if achieving the summit is not your goal.

There is running water for the first third of the hike and patches of shade for the first mile. The last portion doesn't offer much shade and can get hot. Bring plenty of water, especially for the pup. Hiking poles are helpful.

GET MOVING

Locate the pit toilets and information kiosk on the north side of Mill Creek Canyon Road. The Mount Aire Trail sign marks the start and lowest point of elevation, 6640 feet. Begin ascending the well-trodden dirt single track with Elbow Fork creek babbling to the right. Showy goldeneyes, sticky purple geranium, and aspen fleabanes color the forest floor under chokecherries, Oregon boxleaf, and Rocky Mountain maples.

After 0.25 mile, reach the Mount Aire and Lambs Canyon junction. Go left toward Mount Aire, cross a wood footbridge, and move into mature coniferous forest with scattered patches of shade. Come to a junction a few hundred feet after the bridge. Go left (right leads to a stone bench) and then cross another small footbridge.

Arrive at a pristine resting or picnicking wood bench at the base of three enormous white firs at 0.5 mile. Once past the bench, enjoy more consistent shade in stands of quaking aspens, lush thimbleberry bushes, and cone flowers. Around 0.9 mile, the trail becomes rockier.

Before moving out of the Elbow Fork drainage, amble through several steep meadows rioting with arrowleaf balsamroot in blooming months. At 1.1 miles and 7780 feet elevation, gain a saddle and take a welcome break from climbing.

A spectacular mid-summer sunset from the saddle below Mount Aire

Look right to view Mount Aire and the final 800-plus feet of climbing.

At the saddle, go right to begin the exposed ascent. Advance through a series of steep switchbacks. The difficulty of the final push is made a bit easier by the gorgeous scarlet gilia and purple lupines nestled among big sage and Gambel oaks. At the second-to-last switchback, you'll gain a view of Parleys Canyon and I-80. The last few hundred feet are rocky but easy to follow.

The summit, at over 8610 feet in elevation, marks 1.9 miles from the trailhead. Take some time to relish the expansive views. The Park City ridgeline, including Summit Park Peak and Murdock Peak, lies east. The Mill Creek/Big Cottonwood ridgeline to the south showcases Wilson Peak and Gobblers Knob. Mount Olympus (Hike 20) is to the southwest, and an up-close perspective of Grandeur Peak (Hike 15) is due west.

When you're ready, retrace your steps back to the trailhead to complete the 3.8-mile adventure.

GO FARTHER

Tack on a mile (or several) by exploring a portion of the 7.2-mile (one-way) Pipeline Trail (Hike 14). From Elbow Fork, it's just under 3 miles to reach the Burch Hollow trailhead on Pipeline. The 1.5 miles going down the canyon are nearly flat and relatively well-shaded, but the next mile or so approaching Burch Hollow loses 600 feet of elevation. Choose the appropriate distance for you and add a bit of flavor to the already challenging Mount Aire hike.

17 Dog Lake

DISTANCE:	6 miles
ELEVATION GAIN:	1200 feet
HIGH POINT:	8800 feet
DIFFICULTY:	Moderate
TIME:	3 hours
FITNESS:	Hikers, runners
FAMILY-FRIENDLY:	Yes
DOG-FRIENDLY:	Yes, but note that dogs need to be on-leash on even-numbered days.
AMENITIES:	Restrooms at Upper and Lower Big Water trailheads
CONTACT/MAP:	US Forest Service
GPS:	40.68432°N, 111.64689°W
BEFORE YOU GO:	Fee area. Trails open to equestrians. Mountain bikes are permitted on even-numbered days. Seasonal road closure. No cell phone service. For winter travel, avalanche education and equipment are recommended.

GETTING THERE

Driving: From I-215, take exit 4 and go east 0.2 mile on 3900 S. Turn left on Wasatch Boulevard and then right on 3800 S /

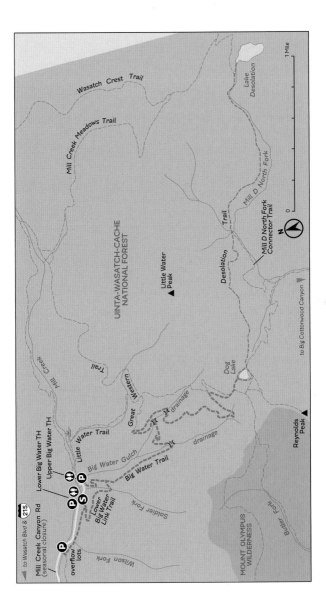

Mill Creek Canyon Road. Drive for 0.7 mile to reach the toll-booth (pay upon exiting) and then continue 8.4 miles until the end of the road to reach Upper Big Water trailhead. There are two additional parking lots below the upper lot. The winter road closure at Maple Grove picnic area adds 2.5 miles walking each way.

Dog Lake is aptly named. Watching doggies flit and frolic in the water is a delight for animal lovers. On hot summer days, the area is especially popular.

The climb to the lake gradually ambles through alternating coniferous and deciduous forests. Pine needles coat the trail beneath the towering spruces, which create a shady, cool climate on north-facing slopes. The trail shifts to dappled shade in aspen forests on the southerly slopes. Midsummer to early fall, the undergrowth bursts with paintbrush, giant fireweed, sticky purple geranium, aspen fleabane, and showy goldeneye.

GET MOVING

There are two access points for Big Water Trail, where the hike begins. If you scored a spot in the upper parking lot, locate the Upper Big Water trailhead (elevation 7600 feet) opposite the restrooms. Then go straight for 0.3 mile to a three-way junction, which meets the leg of Big Water Trail accessed from the two lower parking areas.

If you parked at the Lower Big Water trailhead (elevation 7600 feet), just west of the trailhead look for a large sign and trail map marking the beginning of the hike. Snap a picture of the map since there is no cell phone service. After a few steps, go right at a T intersection and walk a few hundred feet to the Big Water Trail sign, then turn left.

If you parked at the farthest west overflow lot, look for a sign for the Big Water Connector Trail. Follow the connector

Aspen forest turning golden in early fall near Dog Lake

trail for 0.5 mile and gain 160 feet of elevation. Take a sharp right at the Big Water Trail sign (just above the Lower Big Water trailhead).

For both western lots, continue past the Big Water Trail sign on the Lower Big Water Link Trail, a wide, well-worn path. The rich smell of earth emits from the forest floor as you ascend beneath a canopy of towering conifers, gradually gaining 100 feet before the first switchback at 0.25 mile.

Arrive at a signed three-way junction at 0.5 mile from the lower trailhead, where the Big Water Trails converge. Go right to continue up Big Water Trail toward Dog Lake. Immediately after the intersection, enter a small patch of aspen forest. As the trail gently ascends, it shifts back into shade among Engelmann and white spruce. Listen for the nourishing sound of the stream from the canyon below.

Cross a small bridge 1.1 miles from the trailhead (elevation 8000 feet) and continue gradually climbing. Cross a second bridge at 1.5 miles and continue for another 0.2 mile, enjoying views down the canyon, until you reach a signed three-way junction with the Great Western Trail. Turn right here toward Dog Lake.

Reach the final bridge crossing at 2 miles—the creek is often dry here in late summer and early fall. After crossing the bridge, follow the gently winding trail for 0.8 mile, gaining another 400 feet.

Reach a four-way junction with the Little Water Trail; Dog Lake is a quarter mile beyond. From the junction, both right and straight will lead to Dog Lake; go right for the shorter option. Gain the final 130 feet of elevation and reach a three-way junction that meets with the alternative route to Dog Lake. Continue up a short steep section to gain the crest and the 8800-foot high point; from here Dog Lake will be visible. For the final 0.1 mile, the trail gently descends to the shores of Dog Lake. When you're done watching the splashing pooches, return the way you came for a 6-mile roundtrip hike.

GO FARTHER

Explore Desolation Trail, a peaceful path connecting Dog Lake with Lake Desolation, just 2.5 miles away. (Note: Lake Desolation does not allow dogs or horses.)

From the shores of Dog Lake, take the path around the eastern side of the lake. After 0.1 mile, reach a sign indicating the boundary of where animals are permitted. In a few more steps, go left toward Lake Desolation at a signed three-way junction. Enjoy the mostly flat trail as it ambles through stunning aspen meadows. Another three-way intersection pops up at 1.1 miles with the Mill D North Fork Connector; continue straight. Over the next 1.3 miles, the trail gradually gains 500 feet in elevation; the steepest portion comes right before reaching the high point at 9255 feet.

From the high point, the scenery opens up and several paths meander through the meadows. At 2.4 miles, the path forks; take the right fork and trend right for the next 0.1 mile to reach Lake Desolation. Soak up the stunning view—the aspens are a spectacular blaze of gold during the fall.

Next page: *View of southern Salt Lake City from the saddle below the Mount Olympus summit (Hike 20)*

MURRAY, MILLCREEK, AND HOLLADAY

Three rigorous hikes in this section start right out of neighborhoods, including one of the most challenging hikes in this book, Mount Olympus (Hike 20). The crown jewel of Salt Lake, Mount Olympus will reward you with a fresh perspective and an overwhelming sense of awe when gazing up from the valley floor. This massive peak resides in the Mount Olympus Wilderness, which preserves the pristine landscapes around the namesake peak, as well as Neffs Canyon (Hike 19), and Heughs Canyon (Hike 21). The towns of Millcreek and Holladay cleave to the eastern boundary of the Mount Olympus Wilderness. The wilderness peaks and canyons, visible from Murray, are like jewels on the horizon.

Two green spaces within the urban sprawl, Big Cottonwood Regional Park (Hike 18) and Murray Canal and Wheeler Historic Farm (Hike 22), offer excellent views of Neffs Canyon, Heughs Canyon, and Mount Olympus. Neffs Canyon and Heughs Canyon are dog-friendly hikes with free-flowing water and plenty of shade, which make them excellent warm-weather options. The lower-elevation hikes in this area have no avalanche danger and are perfect choices for winter recreation.

18 Big Cottonwood Regional Park

DISTANCE:	4-mile loop
ELEVATION GAIN:	120 feet
HIGH POINT:	4350 feet
DIFFICULTY:	Easy
TIME:	2 hours
FITNESS:	Walkers, runners
FAMILY-FRIENDLY:	Yes, jogger stroller–friendly and ADA-accessible
DOG-FRIENDLY:	Yes, on-leash. Poop bags and waste bins at the parking areas.
AMENITIES:	Restrooms, playground, benches, sports court
CONTACT/MAP:	Salt Lake County Parks and Open Space
GPS:	40.6697˚N, 111.8479˚W
BEFORE YOU GO:	Open dawn to dusk. This trail is also popular with cyclists.

GETTING THERE

Public Transit: Take UTA bus route 45 and get off at Murray Holladay Road / 1635 E. Walk 0.1 mile west to 1590 E and turn right. The parking lot and trail access is 0.2 mile on the right. **Bike Route:** Use the Salt Lake City & County Bikeways Map to plot a route to the trailhead. **Driving:** From I-15, take exit 301 for 4500 S and go east for 1.6 miles. Turn right on 700 E and continue for 0.4 mile until it becomes Van Winkle. Follow Van Winkle another 0.6 mile and then turn left on Murray Holladay Road. After 0.9 mile, turn left on 1590 E. (Note: The 1590 E sign is small and difficult to see; also look for a yellow "dead-end" sign. If you reach the Holladay Lions Recreation Center, you've gone too far.) The parking lot is 0.2 mile on the right.

A **122.5-acre urban green space,** Big Cottonwood Regional Park is comprised of three areas: Big Cottonwood, Creekside, and Holladay Lions. Team sports reign supreme in the Big Cottonwood Area: here you'll find a baseball/softball complex,

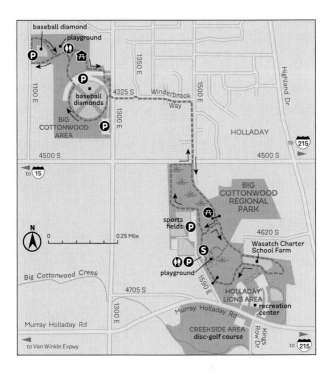

sports field, volleyball court, playground, picnic tables, a pavilion, and 1.7 miles of paved paths. At Creekside, a disc-golf course is the main attraction. The Holladay Lions Area is a quiet space with a small playground, large open fields, and a paved interpretive trail along wetlands. Salt Lake City has a master plan to enlarge the whole park with additional wetland environments and green spaces.

The trail as described here first explores the wide, flat dirt paths within the Holladay Lions Area. Next it follows paved trails through a quiet neighborhood to Big Cottonwood. Dramatic views of Mount Olympus (Hike 20) and the Broads Fork Twin Peaks crown the eastern skyline as you wander the park.

Snow-capped Mount Olympus (Hike 20) as seen from a pleasant winter stroll in Big Cottonwood Regional Park (Hike 18)

GET MOVING

The parking lot faces a playground structure and paved interpretive paths to the east. Locate the wide dirt trail in the northeast corner of the lot and follow it for 300 hundred feet until the trail forks. Take the right fork to stroll under a shady canopy of Russian olive trees, an invasive species. Keep an eye out for milkweed, an essential food source for monarch butterflies. Continue to a junction with a broad paths to the left and the right.

Turn right to begin the 0.75-mile loop around the south end of the Holladay Lions Area. At 0.3 mile, the trail forks; continue straight, walking under some large cottonwood trees to another intersection. This time, turn left off the main track for a 0.3-mile loop around the perimeter of the Wasatch Charter School Farm and beekeeping area. Take a moment to enjoy the dramatic views of the Wasatch Mountains to the east.

At 0.6 mile from the start, turn left when the garden loop regains the main trail. The trail trends right and leads through a gate; keep moving right and walk until you see the restrooms and trailhead parking lot.

The parking area marks the end of the first 0.9-mile loop. To continue the hike, locate the starting point and walk the trail for a second time. When the path forks, this time go straight. The track narrows and veers left to hug a basketball court and then continues north through a grassy field. Blue spruce and willow trees line the trail to the left, and there is a sizeable shrubby area to the right. The grass and shrubby area here can be muddy during winter and spring.

At 1.3 miles, the trail veers right and runs parallel to 4500 S for 0.1 mile. Instead of following the trail back toward the Holladay Lions Area, use the crosswalk to cross 4500 S toward the Big Cottonwood Area. Go north (straight) on 1500 E for 0.2 mile and then turn left on Winderbrook Way, a quaint neighborhood lane. At 1.8 miles, Winderbrook Way veers right and becomes 1350 E; instead of following it right, look for a footpath to 4325 S straight ahead. Take the footpath and continue west for 0.1 mile to reach 1300 E, with a clear view of the Big Cottonwood Area ahead.

Use caution crossing 1300 E; there is no crosswalk. Walk through the parking lot to find a sidewalk that encircles the baseball diamonds at 2 miles. Go left to begin a clockwise loop. Reach a parking lot in 0.2 mile and follow the sidewalk left toward a playground. Start a 0.4-mile loop by veering left toward a baseball field and 1100 E. At 2.5 miles, reach the westernmost parking area. Turn right on 1100 E for 0.1 mile and then go right into the park to complete the loop.

At the playground, follow the path left and climb to the pavilion with picnic tables, horseshoes, hopscotch, and stunning mountain views. From the pavilion, walk down a grassy hill to a sidewalk and then follow the sidewalk to the park entrance at 3 miles.

Cautiously cross 1300 E and retrace the route back on Winderbrook Way and 1500 E. At 3.7 miles from the start, cross 4500 S at the crosswalk and re-enter the Holladay Lions Area on a dirt path. For the next quarter mile, the track meanders between horse pastures on the left and shrubby fields on the right. This area has resident foxes, and they are a delight to watch. Please refrain from feeding them!

Just before a gate, you'll see a beautiful location for a picnic on the right. Pass through the gate and turn right. When the trail forks once more, go left and walk the final few hundred feet back to the starting point to complete your 4-mile saunter.

GO FARTHER

Before returning to the car, explore the short, paved walkways around the wetland area. Read the interpretive signs and relax on benches offering views of pristine wetland scenery, Mount Olympus, and Broads Fork Twin Peaks.

19 Neffs Canyon

DISTANCE:	5.5 miles
ELEVATION GAIN:	2300 feet
HIGH POINT:	7900 feet
DIFFICULTY:	Challenging
TIME:	4 hours
FITNESS:	Hikers
FAMILY-FRIENDLY:	The trail becomes increasingly steep.
DOG-FRIENDLY:	Yes, on-leash. Poop bags and waste bins at the trailhead.
AMENITIES:	Parking, trail map
CONTACT/MAP:	US Forest Service
GPS:	40.67727˚N, 111.77637˚W
BEFORE YOU GO:	Rattlesnake sightings. There is no cell phone service in Neffs Canyon. For winter travel, avalanche education and equipment are recommended.

GETTING THERE

Public Transit: Using public transit adds about 1.8 miles of walking each way. A bike makes the commute easier. Take UTA bus route 45 to Wasatch Boulevard / 4471 S. Head north on Wasatch Boulevard, turn right on E. Oakview Drive, and travel for 0.9 mile. Turn left on Parkview Drive and then right on S 4260 E. Reach White Way and turn right to follow it to the trailhead. **Bike Route:** Use the Salt Lake City & County Bikeways Map to plot a route to the trailhead. **Driving:** From I-215, take exit 4 for 3900 S (southbound) or Wasatch Boulevard (northbound). Travel south on Wasatch Boulevard to reach E. Oakview Drive. Turn left and travel for 0.9 mile. Then turn left on Parkview Drive and right on S 4260 E. Reach White Way and turn right to follow the road until it ends at the trailhead.

Nestled between Mill Creek Canyon (Hikes 14–17) and Mount Olympus (Hike 20), Neffs Canyon is a treasure. A true wilderness hike, you'll ascend into a space unaltered by human

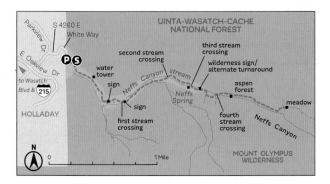

hands. The trailhead is less than 2 miles from a major inter-state, yet the area is still a likely habitat for reclusive mountain creatures like cougars and bears. Seasonal highlights include blossoming wildflowers and the rich hues of fall foliage. The apex is an alpine meadow featuring up-close views of Mount Olympus and Wildcat Ridge.

A popular destination for dog owners, after-work hikers, and weekenders, this trail is a shady, cooler option for hot days. The path follows streams nearly the whole route, crossing Neffs Canyon stream a handful of times. There are no bridges—wear shoes you don't mind getting wet and consider bring hiking poles for creek crossings. A plethora of unofficial social trails have cropped up along the route; keep to the established trail up to the meadow. Dense vegetation can mean a lot of bugs. If it's snowy, bring micro-traction spikes.

GET MOVING

From the southeast corner of the parking area, locate the trail sign and map marking the beginning of the route and the lowest point of elevation, 5600 feet. Take in views of Mount Olympus and its acclaimed alpine climbing route, *The West Slabs*, to the south. Follow the path to the right of the sign up a well-worn single track and soon reach a T intersection. Go right and begin a steady climb up a wide, gravel double track.

Lush meadows and a view of Mount Olympus near the Neffs Canyon trailhead

The first 0.5 mile is the most exposed—the Gambel oaks and bigtooth maples bordering the trail provide little to no shade. Many unofficial trails intersect the main path; stay on the double track to keep on the correct route. Pass a water tower at 0.3 mile. Around half a mile in, you'll begin to hear the watercourse, and soon after, the trail encounters Neffs Canyon stream at a signed junction (elevation 5930 feet).

Follow the arrow on the sign and go left at the fork; after the turn, the double track narrows to a dirt trail. Big sagebrush, Woods' rose, and grasses give way to denser vegetation as you parallel the stream. For the next couple of miles, mature white firs, Fremont cottonwoods, box elders, willows, and chokecherry shade most of the ascent. During wildflower season, the trail is a cornucopia of colored petals. As the path meanders near the gurgling water, look for Wasatch beard-tongue, arrowleaf balsamroot, scarlet gilia, twolobe larkspur, bluebells, and Oregon grape.

The next 0.1 mile can be wet or icy as it climbs next to the watercourse. Cross the stream at 0.7 mile. When the trail forks again at 0.8 mile, follow the directional sign and head left. Ignore unofficial trails; follow the signs and stay on the most well-worn path.

As you ascend, the trail becomes increasingly steep and less populated. Cross a drainage about 1.25 miles in, just before a second notable stream crossing. The third major stream crossing is at 1.5 miles, with Neffs Spring to the right. After that, the way gets even steeper and rockier until it encounters the Mount Olympus Wilderness sign at 1.6 miles (elevation 6670 feet). The wilderness sign is a good turn-around point for a more moderate, 3.2-mile adventure.

Shortly after the wilderness sign, the trail becomes even more unruly. At 1.8 miles, keep left at the fork. Encounter the most notable and challenging stream crossing at around 2 miles. This is a tricky spot—there is a misleading unofficial trail that steeply ascends to the right. Don't take this alluring path; to stay on the correct route, carefully cross the stream. The water is typically no more than a foot deep; however, it's fast-moving in this narrow section. Once on the other side, the trail is easily distinguishable as it abruptly climbs next to the fast-flowing water.

Shortly after the major stream crossing, encounter a delightful aspen forest. Gorgeous flora—including many-flower stickseed, Richardson's geranium, smallflower wood-land star, and late-season yellow avalanche-lilies—help the next 800 feet of elevation gain whiz past.

At 2.75 miles, the aspen forest opens to a superb high-alpine meadow nestled under Wildcat Ridge and South Thayne Peak. Soon after, reach a fork in the trail at the route's high point (elevation 7900 feet) and go right. Wander a few hundred feet and find a place to bask under the quartzite cliffs, a perfect reward for the strenuous climb. (Past the meadow, the trail continues and eventually gains the ridge between Mill Creek Canyon and Big Cottonwood Canyon.)

After reveling in high-meadow beauty, retrace your steps back to the trailhead to complete the 5.5-mile excursion.

20 Mount Olympus

DISTANCE:	7 miles
ELEVATION GAIN:	3600 feet
HIGH POINT:	8420 feet
DIFFICULTY:	Challenging
TIME:	6 hours
FITNESS:	Hikers
FAMILY-FRIENDLY:	Steep and challenging. Suitable for older children or walking a portion of the hike with young children.
DOG-FRIENDLY:	Yes, on-leash. Poop bags and waste bins at the trailhead.
AMENITIES:	Parking, restrooms
CONTACT/MAP:	US Forest Service
GPS:	40.65310°N, 111.80642°W
BEFORE YOU GO:	Mostly exposed and very hot during the summer months. Wildflowers from spring through summer. Frequent rattlesnake sightings. For winter travel, avalanche education and equipment are recommended.

GETTING THERE

Public Transit: Taking the bus adds 2.4 miles of walking each way. A bike makes the commute easier. Take UTA bus route 223 and get off on 3000 E / 6518 S. Then consult the Salt Lake City & County Bikeways Map. **Bike Route:** Use the Salt Lake City & County Bikeways Map to plot a route to the trail-head. **Driving:** From I-215, take exit 6 for UT 190. Head east on 6200 S / UT 190 for 0.7 mile. Turn left on Wasatch Boulevard

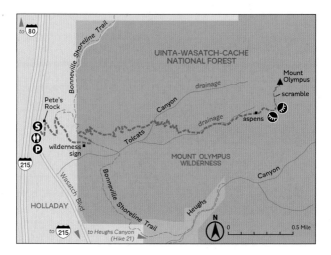

and travel for 1.7 miles to the Mount Olympus trailhead on the right.

With its jagged quartzite summit, Mount Olympus is Salt Lake City's most dominant peak—it's visible from most places in the valley. While *The West Slabs*, *Kamp's Ridge*, and *Geurt's Ridge* are favorite climbing routes, the robust hike described here is great for those without advanced rock-climbing skills. It's also ideal for athletic conditioning—the staggering 3600-foot elevation gain in 3.5 miles makes Mount Olympus one of the most challenging hikes in this book. Reaching the viewpoint is an applaudable goal; however, hiking only a portion of the trail is also an excellent way to build up your fitness.

As the rigorous route progresses, there are countless opportunities to observe nature's diversity—the mountain ecology morphs from heat-loving plants like sages and curl-leaf mountain mahogany to dense flowering shrubs to a coniferous forest. Debatably, the best reward for hiking Mount Olympus is an immense sense of accomplishment, and a feeling of intimacy when you gaze at the behemoth from below.

Most of the summit trail lies within the Mount Olympus Wilderness.

Autumn is an excellent season for the hike, with cooler temps and colorful foliage. In summer, there is almost no shade by midday—start early and bring a lot of water, three liters or more per person. During spring, be prepared to encounter snow at higher elevations. Winter travel makes the journey much more challenging; hiking to the viewpoint is not advised.

Each year, a surprising number of people get lost on this hike, even though the trail is straightforward. It's a good idea to download or bring a map and stick to the well-worn main path. With dozens of wildflower species and flowering shrubs, there are many insects, so long sleeves and pants are advisable—and hiking poles are helpful in all seasons.

The 7-mile, 3600-foot-elevation-gain trek described here climbs up to a saddle with an excellent viewpoint. However, the actual summit (see Go Farther) requires Class 3 scrambling to gain 600 feet in 0.4 mile.

GET MOVING

Locate the restrooms and a metal gate marking the start; the trailhead is the lowest elevation point of the hike at 4820 feet. Follow the pavement for a few dozen feet until it becomes dirt. Stick to the well-defined main path; shortcuts are blocked off, especially near the beginning. The enormous boulder at 0.3 mile is named Pete's Rock in honor of climbing community pioneer Christian O'Dell "Pete" Petersen.

Encounter the signed Bonneville Shoreline Trail at 0.6 mile and go right. Next, look for the Mount Olympus Wilderness sign at 0.9 mile. Reach another Bonneville Shoreline Trail sign at 1 mile and go left (right goes to Heughs Canyon, Hike 21). By this time, you've gained 700 feet of elevation. At 1.1 miles, come to the final Bonneville Shoreline Trail connection; keep right.

Scattered juniper stands offer occasional shade, and heat-loving plants like Gambel oak, white sage, rabbitbrush, arrowleaf balsamroot, and yarrow line the path leading to the seasonal watercourse.

The drainage at 2 miles is a welcome shady reprieve. When the water is flowing, this is a favorite place for dogs to cool off. The creek's elevation is 6280 feet, which means there are more than 2000 vertical feet to climb in the next 1.5 miles. Take a rest here under the shade of mature bigtooth maples, Utah serviceberries, and chokecherry trees.

Cross a second drainage (typically dry) at 2.75 miles and 7080 feet elevation. The next 0.75 mile is incredibly steep and rocky, gaining over 1300 feet in elevation. Fortunately, wildflowers and an abundance of wildlife make the ascent more bearable.

Fernleaf biscuitroot, Pacific ninebark, and snowberry shrubs bloom with delicate, creamy, bright-white flower clusters. Twolobe larkspur, tapertip onions, diamond clarkia, three-nerve fleabane, and Whipple's penstemon speckle the landscape with violet, lilac, and lavender and are complemented by the vibrant golden-yellows of radiant tapertip hawksbeard, wall-flower, yellow salsify, and blooming stonecrop. Deciduous trees give way to a coniferous forest of towering white firs. A stand of aspens appears when the climb is nearly over.

Avoid shortcuts that erode terrain—keep on the well-defined, rocky scramble. At 3.5 miles, after an intense climb, the site of level land is a welcome relief. Reach the first of two viewpoints at the hike's high point (elevation 8420 feet). The second view is a few dozen feet beyond. Take a well-deserved break and refuel while soaking up the astonishing scenery. To the south, Heughs Canyon is straight below. Storm Mountain, the Pfeifferhorn, upper Bells Canyon (lower Bells Canyon is Hike 28), and Lone Peak sweep the skyline.

When you're ready, retrace your steps back to the trail-head to complete the 7-mile journey.

GO FARTHER

The 0.4-mile, 600-foot-elevation-gain scramble to the peak is an adventure. The path through the rocks is well-defined; however, some folks may want to hire a guiding service to feel secure on the Class 3 terrain.

To climb to the peak, continue from the second viewpoint, following the main trail until it encounters a rocky, steep ascent. Follow the path of least resistance up. Keep in mind that ascending is easier than descending—if going down isn't going to be possible, do not go up! This is a heavily trafficked Class 3 scramble, so no bushwhacking is required.

Views from the peak are majestic. When you're back down in the valley, you'll be able to look up at Mount Olympus and know firsthand what it's like to be on the summit.

21 Heughs Canyon

DISTANCE:	3.1 miles
ELEVATION GAIN:	1240 feet
HIGH POINT:	6100 feet
DIFFICULTY:	Challenging
TIME:	3 hours
FITNESS:	Hikers
FAMILY-FRIENDLY:	Yes
DOG-FRIENDLY:	Yes, on-leash. Pack out waste.
AMENITIES:	Parking
CONTACT/MAP:	Bonneville Shoreline Trail
GPS:	40.63685°N, 111.79786°W
BEFORE YOU GO:	The waterfall and wildflowers are most spectacular in spring and early summer. Vehicle break-ins are common at the trailhead. Frequent rattlesnake sightings. Popular evening hike. For winter travel, avalanche education and equipment are recommended.

GETTING THERE

Public Transit: Taking the bus adds about 1.2 miles of walking each way. A bike makes the commute easier. Take UTA bus route 223 and get off on 3000 E / 6518 S. Go north on 3000 E to the Hyatt Place hotel. Turn right and skirt the southern perimeter of the hotel. Then turn left on 3170 E and follow it as it curves right. Take the footpath parallel to busy 6200 S and travel southeast for 0.4 mile. At the Wasatch Boulevard intersection, turn left to cross 6200 S. Walk north on Wasatch Boulevard for 0.5 mile, and look for the Heughs Canyon Trail sign and parking on the right. **Bike Route:** Use the Salt Lake City & County Bikeways Map to plot a route to the trailhead. **Driving:** From I-215, take exit 6 for 6200 S / UT 190. Head east off the exit on 6200 S / UT 190 for 0.7 mile. Turn left on Wasatch Boulevard and go north for 0.5 mile. The Heughs Canyon Trail sign and six parking spots are on the right. If the spots are full, park along Wasatch Boulevard. Access to the

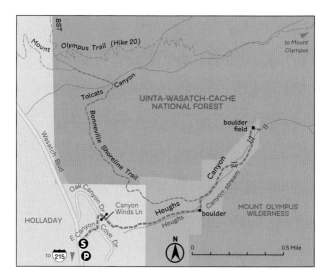

canyon is through a neighborhood. Be respectful of people's homes and property—park in designated areas.

Heughs Canyon Trail is a gem. Hike through lush vegetation as the liquid purl of a wilderness creek drowns out any city noise and Mount Olympus looms above you. The majority of the trail runs parallel to Heughs Canyon's stream and eventually ends at a hidden waterfall. A short scramble over boulders leads to the majestic cascade, which transforms throughout the seasons: wild ice sculptures during the winter, a raging flow in late spring and early summer, and a gentle trickle come fall. Mature trees and dense foliage near the flowing water create a shady and cool reprieve on hot summer days.

During spring runoff or high-water periods, the path may have wet patches. Hiking poles are helpful in all seasons. During the cold months, the trail can be icy; micro-traction spikes are recommended.

Wildflowers line the shady path in Heughs Canyon.

GET MOVING

The trickiest part of the hike is finding the neighborhood trailhead. The trail starts at the lowest elevation point, 4860 feet, at the signed Heughs Canyon Trail parking area on Wasatch

Boulevard. From the parking area, walk north a few hundred feet to East Canyon Cove Drive and turn right. Continue for 0.2 mile to Oak Canyon Drive and turn left. When you reach Canyon Winds Lane, turn right. Look for a footpath to the right of a large gate and follow it until it dead-ends, 0.4 mile from the start.

The pavement becomes a wide dirt path that quickly narrows. Within several hundred feet, the gurgling creek brings a drastic change of scenery. Chokecherry and western serviceberry trees sparkle with seasonal white blooms. White firs and poplars tower above the trail, while canyon maples and Gambel oaks glow burnt orange and red in autumn.

Just before 1 mile, look for a boulder to the right. Scramble up it to enjoy a stunning view of quartzite cliffs surrounding the summit of Mount Olympus (Hike 20). After climbing nearly 700 feet in 1 mile, reach a signed junction for the Bonneville Shoreline Trail (see Go Farther). Go straight to continue up Heughs Canyon.

Abundant wildflowers please the eye and feed the soul. Look for the fragrant yellow blossoms of Oregon grape, pink and red wild roses, and the eye-catching purple blooms of the non-native silver dollar plant.

Cross the creek on a wood footbridge at 1.3 miles and then a second footbridge after a short distance. The trail becomes very steep and rocky before ending at a large boulder field at 1.5 miles. When the path ends, the top of the waterfall is visible to the south.

Getting to the waterfall requires several hundred feet of boulder scrambling. Locate the top of the waterfall, choose a landmark, and move south (not up) across the boulders on the path of least resistance. Boulder hopping can be challenging, especially for dogs, but the waterfall view is well worth the effort.

Enjoy the falls. When you're ready to head home, retrace your route back to the parking area to complete your 3.1-mile adventure.

GO FARTHER

The 1.5-mile portion of the BST that connects Heughs Canyon Trail to the Mount Olympus Trail offers a refreshing perspective, with scenery and ecology noticeably different from
Heughs Canyon. Follow the route described here to tack on a
few (mostly flat) miles, losing and gaining less than 200 feet
as you traverse the west-facing slope.

From the Bonneville Shoreline Trail sign near the large
boulder, go north on the well-defined trail. After a few hundred feet, the path moves away from the water; for the rest of
the route, Gambel oak and white sage line the shadeless dirt
path. Enjoy expansive views of Salt Lake City and the Oquirrh
Mountains, including Blackridge (Hike 42) and Oquirrh Lake
Loop (Hike 41) to the west. Just before the finishing point,
catch a stunning glimpse of Mount Olympus's peak. After Tol-
cats Canyon, cross a couple of small talus fields.

The turnaround point is where the BST intercepts the
Mount Olympus Trail. Retrace your steps back to the trail sign
to complete the 3-mile roundtrip addition.

---

22 Murray Canal and Wheeler Historic Farm

DISTANCE:	4.2 miles
ELEVATION GAIN:	80 feet
HIGH POINT:	4400 feet
DIFFICULTY:	Easy
TIME:	2 hours
FITNESS:	Walkers, runners
FAMILY-FRIENDLY:	An excellent choice for families. Stroller- and ADA-accessible gravel and paved paths (all-terrain wheels helpful). Farm animals and activities.
DOG-FRIENDLY:	Yes, on-leash. Poop bags and waste bins in park.

AMENITIES: Parking, restrooms, pavilion, playground, picnic tables, historical structures, interpretive signs, visitor center, farm store, farm animals, activities, seasonal farmers' market

CONTACT/MAP: Murray City Parks and Recreation (Murray Canal); Salt Lake County Parks and Open Space (Wheeler Historic Farm)

GPS: 40.63450°N, 111.86431°W

BEFORE YOU GO: Murray Canal Trail hours are 6:00 AM to 11:00 PM, and it is popular with cyclists. Wheeler Historic Farm hours are dawn to dusk. Stop by the information office in the activity barn for maps and park details. Wheeler Historic Farm is a popular destination year-round.

GETTING THERE

Public Transit: Take UTA bus route 209 and get off at 900 E Southwood Drive. The bus stop is at the north entrance of Wheeler Historic Farm. Walk south to the southern parking area and trailhead. **Bike Route:** Use the Salt Lake City & County Bikeways Map to plot a route to the trail. **Driving:** From I-215, take exit 9 for Union Park Avenue. Go north on Union Park Avenue, take an immediate left on 6600 S, and travel for 0.2 mile. Turn right on 900 E and go for 0.1 mile to the Wheeler Historic Farm south entrance. Turn right into the park and follow the road to the southern parking area.

Wheeler Historic Farm makes for a delightful family outing or urban stroll. The 75-acre property operated as a farm for over a hundred years. When Salt Lake County purchased it in 1969, they initially planned to tear down the old buildings to develop a regional park. Fortunately, in 1974, the Junior League of Salt Lake City approached Salt Lake County with a well-researched plan to repair the historical structures and preserve the space as a working historical farm. In 1976, Wheeler Historic Farm opened for public enjoyment. Walking around the farm and participating in activities can fill a whole

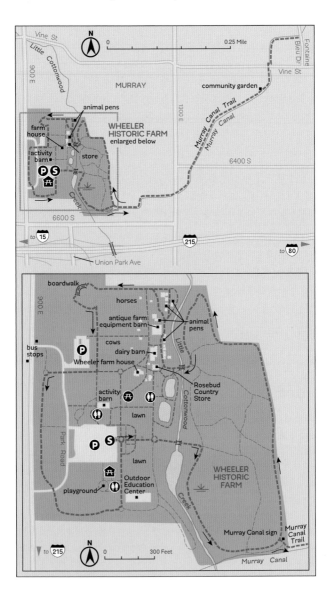

day. Plan for time to explore the historical structures and visit the animals (see Go Further).

Easy access to the 2.4-mile out-and-back Murray Canal Trail makes for a pleasant bonus trek. Enjoy the birds and flowers along the canal trail and then return to loop around Wheeler Historic Farm. The terrain is primarily flat and varies from pavement to gravel to dirt.

GET MOVING

From the southern parking area, head east on the paved path between the signed central lawn and the south lawn. In 0.1 mile, the pavement becomes a wide, flat dirt path that crosses Little Cottonwood Creek on a footbridge. After a few hundred feet, reach an intersection, and go right.

The trail wanders next to the creek in a designated wetland environment for the next 0.25 mile. Several beaches and scattered benches create a perfect setting to soak in the creekside sounds and sights. Enormous Fremont cottonwood, box elder, Russian olive (invasive), and Siberian elm (invasive) trees create an inviting shade canopy on hot days.

At a three-way junction, go straight. Look for the Murray Canal Trail sign at 0.4 mile and turn right onto the canal. This sign marks the beginning of the 2.4-mile out-and-back pedestrian passage. The canal is home to many bird species, including a large population of mallards. During the blooming season, the trail's perimeter bursts with Woods' roses, wildflowers, and grasses (unfortunately, many species are invasive).

Reach a large community garden on the left and find a remarkable view of Mount Olympus (Hike 20) and one of its alpine climbing routes, *Geurt's Ridge*. The road crossing on Vine Street just past the community garden marks the highest point of elevation at 4400 feet. Arrive at the end of the Murray Canal Trail at Fontaine Bleu Drive. Turn around here

Wheeler Historic Farm includes dozens of restored farm structures and exhibits.

and retrace your steps. You'll reach the Murray Canal Trail sign again at 2.8 miles.

The remaining 1.4 miles follows a wonky, counterclockwise loop around the perimeter of Wheeler Historic Farm. From the Murray Canal Trail sign, go right on the wide gravel path to explore the natural area. Mature trees and a blanket of emerald grasses foster a feeling of wilderness, making the proximity of urban life hard to believe.

Over the next 0.3 mile, the path forks several times. At each fork, veer right. At 3.1 miles from the start, you'll reach an intersection with a narrow footpath on the right leading to Little Cottonwood Creek and a shady streamside beach. Turn right onto the footpath, follow it past the beach until it reaches a T intersection, and then go right to cross Little Cottonwood Creek on a footbridge.

From here, the trail leads straight into the heart of the historic farm (see Go Further). Turn right after the bridge and walk past farm animals and antique farming equipment. When the trail forks at 3.5 miles, go left. Then in a few hundred feet, go right to enter a forest with a short, aesthetic board-walk. At the end of the boardwalk, go left on a short, narrow dirt path until it encounters the main path. Go right, toward the activity barn, and then at 3.7 miles, at a four-way intersection, go right, walking away from the farmhouse.

To complete the final 0.5 mile of the loop, follow the walkway as it hugs the west and south perimeter of the farm. Veer right at the fork near the playground and walk around the Outdoor Education Center. At 4.2 miles, the track returns to the start, with the parking lot visible to the left.

GO FARTHER

Explore the grounds of Wheeler Historic Farm to witness a working farm that also features antique farming equipment and historical exhibits.

First, stop by the activity barn for maps, event information, and to purchase tokens for wagon rides, milking demonstrations, or farmhouse tours ($1–$4). Don't forget to visit the second floor of the activity barn to see rotating exhibits about the history of farming.

Next, visit the Rosebud Country Store/Blacksmith Shop for refreshments or a Utah-sourced gift. Check out the antique farm equipment barn or take a one-hour tour of the impressive Victorian farmhouse, which is now a museum with over six thousand historical artifacts.

As you meander, look for the horses, cows, pigs, chickens, turkeys, peacocks, rabbits, vegetable gardens, and groves of fruit trees that comprise the working farm. For scrumptious local foods, stop by the Wheeler Sunday Market, where vendors sell Utah-grown produce, baked goods, artisan foods, and gifts (9:00 AM to 1:00 PM, mid-May to mid-October).

Next page: *Salt Lake City, as seen from Ferguson Canyon (Hike 24)*

COTTONWOOD HEIGHTS AND SANDY

Cottonwood Heights and Sandy line the western perimeters of Twin Peaks Wilderness and Lone Peak Wilderness, where countless wild adventures await. Explore a deep granite canyon along a free-flowing creek in Ferguson Canyon (Hike 24) or visit Bells Canyon (Hike 28) and steeply climb to an awe-inspiring waterfall. You can bring the whole family to the paved, mellow Big Cottonwood Canyon Trail (Hike 23) for choice mountain views and a large dose of homesteading history.

At Dimple Dell (Hikes 26 and 27), the largest natural space within Salt Lake's urban footprint, archaeologists have unearthed artifacts dating back millennia. The continued preservation of the area is critical for historical purposes. Its lower elevation and easy public transportation access make Dimple Dell a good choice year-round, but it's especially inviting during snowy months when canyon hikes are more difficult to access.

23 Big Cottonwood Canyon Trail

DISTANCE:	4 miles
ELEVATION GAIN:	350 feet
HIGH POINT:	4920 feet
DIFFICULTY:	Easy
TIME:	2 hours
FITNESS:	Walkers, runners
FAMILY-FRIENDLY:	Yes, paved pathway is suitable for strollers and ADA-accessible. Popular with cyclists.
DOG-FRIENDLY:	Yes, on-leash. Poop bags and waste bins throughout.
AMENITIES:	Parking, restrooms, interpretive signs; picnic area and playground at Knudsen Park
CONTACT/MAP:	Cottonwood Heights Parks and Recreation
GPS:	40.61962˚N, 111.78821˚W
BEFORE YOU GO:	Knudsen Park's hours are 7:00 AM to 10:00 PM.

GETTING THERE

Public Transit: Take UTA bus route 223 and get off at Holladay Boulevard / 6100 S. Walk south on Holladay Boulevard for 0.3 mile to the entrance of Knudsen Park. Walk to the park's southern perimeter to start on Big Cottonwood Canyon Trail. When the ski bus runs, take UTA bus route 953 and get off at the Big Cottonwood Canyon Park and Ride. **Bike Route:** Use the Salt Lake City & County Bikeways Map to plot a route to the trailhead. **Driving:** From I-215, take exit 6 for UT 190 E and travel southeast for 1.6 miles. Turn left on Big Cottonwood Canyon Road. Turn left into Big Cottonwood Canyon Park and Ride, where the trail begins. The park and ride is often full during the ski season, especially on the weekends. Consider parking at Knudsen Park for an alternative start.

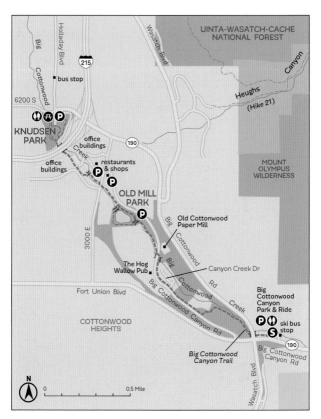

More than a dozen interpretive signs along Big Cottonwood Canyon Trail illustrate the life of the settlers who arrived in Utah in the mid-1800s. As you walk the paved pedestrian path, read historical plaques describing decades of history. Some of the material covered includes the lumber industry, recognition of the contributions of Black pioneers, icehouses and pond use, the Latter-Day Saints tithing house, mining, and the Butler Brewery and Hotel.

The Old Cottonwood Papermill is one of the many historical sites along the Big Cottonwood Canyon Trail.

Begin at Big Cottonwood Canyon Park and Ride and meander next to Big Cottonwood Creek through the scattered shade of common chokecherry, bigtooth maple, and Gambel oak. Then move through a patchwork of homes and ranchlands to an impressive historical stone building. Parallel to the creek, the path strolls through corporate facilities, restaurants, shops, and homes before ending at Knudsen Park.

This trail is not the best for scorching-hot days due to the dark pavement and inconsistent shade. However, the pavement and minimal elevation gain make it a great winter hiking choice; note that some sections might be icy.

GET MOVING

Locate the paved path next to the creek in the northwest corner of the park and ride. The pedestrian trail starts at the highest point of the hike, elevation 4920 feet. Follow a short descent to go through an underpass below Wasatch Boulevard. For the first 0.4 mile, the pathway hugs Big Cottonwood Creek and the gurgling water drowns out the traffic sounds.

At 0.4 mile, the path moves left and away from the creek. A short while later, it veers right, becomes a sidewalk, and proceeds along quiet Big Cottonwood Canyon Road. Cross Canyon Creek Drive at a crosswalk at 0.75 mile and then continue straight on Big Cottonwood Canyon Trail. Keep an eye out for an iconic bar, The Hog Wallow Pub, on your left.

Cross the creek on a bridge at 1 mile (elevation 4720 feet) and use the crosswalk to pick up Big Cottonwood Canyon Trail on the opposite side of Big Cottonwood Canyon Road. The footpath parallels the creek and passes an impressive historical stone structure, the Old Cottonwood Paper Mill. Utah's first established newspaper, the *Deseret News* (still in print today), built the paper mill in 1883. The mill was destroyed by a fire in 1893 and remained defunct until it was rebuilt in 1927 by a private citizen, J. B. Walker. It was central to the local social scene as an open-air dance hall until the onset of World War II.

Stroll under the shady canopy of mature trees for the next quarter mile. Several benches and ample avian activity make this a perfect spot to rest and observe the flourishing biodiversity around the creek. At 1.25 miles reach Old Mill Park, which includes a parking area and a pond. When the trail forks, trend right to stay on the paved Big Cottonwood Canyon Trail (the path around the pond is the Go Farther route).

At 1.5 miles, the path comes to a business park with restaurants and shops; this is a great place to grab snacks or picnic supplies to take to Knudsen Park. Use the pedestrian light to cross 3000 E and go right for a few hundred feet. Look for a sign indicating Big Cottonwood Canyon Trail, turn left, and walk under a dense canopy of bigtooth maples.

Cross the creek on a paved bridge at 1.6 miles. Continue past office buildings for 0.2 mile, follow the path to an I-215 underpass, and then cross the creek on another paved bridge. Big Cottonwood Canyon Trail ends at Knudsen Park (elevation 4580 feet).

Plan to meander quaint Knudsen Park or find a peaceful place to picnic. The park is especially delightful in spring, with Japanese cherry, Callery pear, and cherry plum trees unfurling their pink and white blossoms.

When you're ready, retrace your steps to return to the park and ride and complete your 4-mile roundtrip walk.

GO FARTHER

To add a pleasant 0.2-mile loop to the journey, take a stroll around the pond at Old Mill Park. Look for the pond 0.7 mile after leaving Knudsen Park and turn right on a dirt path. Circle the pond to reach a beautiful wooden bridge. To return to the trailhead at the park and ride, cross the bridge and turn right on Big Cottonwood Canyon Trail.

24 **Ferguson Canyon**

DISTANCE:	4 miles
ELEVATION GAIN:	1470 feet
HIGH POINT:	6700 feet
DIFFICULTY:	Challenging
TIME:	2.5 hours
FITNESS:	Hikers
FAMILY-FRIENDLY:	Suitable for older children; the trail is steep.
DOG-FRIENDLY:	Yes, on-leash. Waste bins at the trailhead.
AMENITIES:	Parking, benches, drinking fountain, amphitheater
CONTACT/MAP:	US Forest Service
GPS:	40.61022°N, 111.78827°W
BEFORE YOU GO:	The canyon is closed from 10:00 PM to 6:00 AM. It can be crowded on weekends and evenings. For winter travel, avalanche education and equipment are recommended.

GETTING THERE

Public Transit: Public transit adds about 2 miles of walking each way. A bike makes the commute easier. Take UTA bus route 72 and get off on 3000 E / 6967 S. Then consult the Salt Lake City & County Bikeways Map. **Bike Route:** Use the Salt Lake City & County Bikeways Map to plot a route to the trailhead. **Driving:** From I-215, take exit 6 for 6200 S / UT 190 / Wasatch Boulevard and go south on UT 190 / 6200 S for 1.8 miles. Reach the Big Cottonwood Canyon Road intersection and continue straight on UT 210 for 0.3 mile. Turn left on Prospector Drive, followed by an immediate right to stay on Prospector Drive. Look for an overflow parking lot on the right. Continue another 0.3 mile to Timberline Drive and turn left; the two trailhead parking lots are on the right. If trailhead parking is full, park in the overflow lot on Prospector Drive.

Ferguson Canyon offers a shady escape from the city heat. It's surrounded by a watershed and is one of the few mountainous

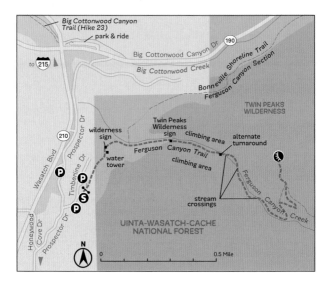

hikes in the area where dogs are welcome. Pups love to flit and play in the small stream. This popular hike starts on a mellow and completely exposed double track—typically hot during the summer—but within a third of a mile, the trail dips into the canyon and the temperature dives. Ferguson Canyon's creek can flow year-round, although the lower sections might be dry in midsummer.

Hike to a popular climbing area, a lovely place for a picnic or a rest amid towering box elders and bigtooth maples. If you want to make it a shorter outing, you can turn around here for a 1.6-mile roundtrip walk.

Plan for seasonal wet areas, which may attract wasps during the summer or generate ice patches during cold months. Parts of the trail are incredibly steep; hiking poles are helpful. During winter, be sure to pack appropriate clothing for colder temps in the canyon; micro-traction spikes and hiking poles are often necessary due to ice accumulation.

Hikers enjoy fall temperatures and the mellow grade near the Ferguson Canyon trailhead.

GET MOVING

Start on the double-track dirt path from the lower parking lot and go northeast for a few hundred feet to pass through gate. This short, shadeless section amid big sage and rabbitbrush offers expansive views of Salt Lake Valley and the Oquirrh Mountains to the west.

At 0.3 mile, the trail hugs a fence and moves to the left of a water tower. Avoid the numerous side paths and stay on the well-worn main trail. Just past the water tower, the trail narrows at a wilderness sign and begins a short descent through Gambel oaks before starting to climb. The Bonneville Shoreline Trail intercepts the route on the left at 0.4 mile; continue straight.

As the forest becomes taller and more diverse, the temperature drops noticeably. Flowering shrubs like chokecherry, Pacific ninebark, and Woods' rose paint the foliage with splashes of white and pink during late spring and early summer. At 0.6 mile, pass a Twin Peaks Wilderness/Wasatch National Forest sign, with granite cliffs hovering above.

After a few hundred feet, the canyon narrows and encounters the first climbing route. Meander along a shady path as it follows the base of the cliffs through climbing areas. Keep an eye out for shiny bolts on the cliffs that indicate a rock climbing route. If watching climbers inspires you, consider giving it a try (see Go Further).

Ignore the numerous side paths around the climbing areas and stick to the well-worn main path. If the trail ends abruptly at a cliff or starts to require bushwhacking, you've lost the way; turn back and locate the main path. At 0.8 mile, the trail steepens considerably and climbs parallel to the drainage.

Cross the drainage and a small stream at 1 mile and 520 vertical feet from the trailhead. Although there is no bridge, it's often possible to make it across without getting wet feet. Even if you didn't see water flowing in the seasonal creek before this area, it's likely there will be running water upstream.

Gain almost 200 feet of elevation in the next 0.2 mile on a gruesome, dusty climb. While this section is extremely steep, it's also short, and making small switchbacks across the wide dirt path will make both the ascent and descent easier. The creek is now to the right, and about halfway up the steep section, a rippling cascade offers a welcome break. Cross the stream again at 1.2 miles and continue to climb.

This next section is typically the wettest. As a result, there may be wasps or ice. On the plus side, hundreds of thimbleberry bushes line the trail and make for yummy seasonal snacking.

Encounter the final stream crossing at 1.5 miles (elevation 6180 feet). The trail veers left 0.25 mile after the third stream crossing and climbs away from the shady drainage.

After a short distance, the trail opens and comes to a fork—both directions lead to the view. Take the less intimidating and more established route to the right. At 1.8 miles, before the last switchback, a double-spire peak called the Hounds Tooth comes into view.

The grade backs off for the final 0.1 mile; enjoy a flat traverse passing occasional curl-leaf mountain mahogany trees. Just after the trail gets flatter, watch for a fork where the trail goes straight or makes a hard right. Go straight to reach the overlook. The viewpoint is just past a large granite outcropping on the left.

The overlook marks the highest point of elevation at 6700 feet. Take in expansive views of Salt Lake City and the surrounding mountains. Mount Olympus (Hike 20), Mount Raymond, and Wildcat Ridge dominate the northern skyline, while the Oquirrh Mountains, Oquirrh Lake (Hike 41), and Blackridge (Hike 42) lie to the west.

Retrace the route to return to the trailhead and complete your 4-mile trek.

GO FURTHER

Ferguson Canyon is one of numerous climbing areas scattered around Salt Lake City. As the hiking trail skirts below the crag through the climbing zone, it's fun to watch climbers scaling the towering granite cliffs. For outdoor lovers seeking a challenge beyond the hiking trail, rock climbing is a great option.

Climbing requires special knowledge and a whole quiver of gear. The safest way to give it a try is to train at a climbing gym or to hire a professional to teach you outdoors. Fortunately, there are countless climbing walls and mountain-guide operations based in and around Salt Lake City. Most guide outfitters will allow you to rent all of the necessary gear. Look for organizations with American Mountain Guide Association (AMGA) certification to ensure your guide has undergone extensive training.

25   Quail Hollow

DISTANCE:	3 miles
ELEVATION GAIN:	150 feet
HIGH POINT:	5090 feet
DIFFICULTY:	Easy to moderate
TIME:	2 hours
FITNESS:	Walkers, hikers, runners
FAMILY-FRIENDLY:	Yes
DOG-FRIENDLY:	Yes, on-leash with restrictions. Dogs are prohibited outside of Quail Hollow on the portion of the hike along Little Cottonwood Creek, which is Salt Lake City's watershed and water source. Poop bags and waste bins at trailhead.
AMENITIES:	Parking
CONTACT/MAP:	Sandy City Parks and Recreation
GPS:	40.58305˚N, 111.80703˚W
BEFORE YOU GO:	Park hours are from dawn to 10:00 PM. The northern portion is popular with mountain bikers.

GETTING THERE

Public Transit: Take UTA bus route F94 and get off at Peacock Drive / 9280 S. Go south on Peacock Drive to Woodchuck Way and turn left. In about 0.2 mile, turn right on Quail Hollow Drive. Take an almost immediate left on Durban Road and continue for 0.4 mile. Go right on Belfair Road and walk a few hundred feet to the winter gate. **Bike Route:** Use the Salt Lake City & County Bikeways Map to plot a route to the trailhead. **Driving:** From I-15, take exit 295 for UT 209 / 9000 S. Go east on 9000 S for 2 miles and continue another 2 miles after the road curves and becomes 9400 S. Turn left on Quail Hollow Drive. In 0.6 mile, turn right on Durban Road. When you reach Belfair Road, turn right, pass through a gate where the road turns to gravel, and follow it to a sizeable seasonal parking area (closed October 15 to April 15). When this lot is closed, park on Belfair Road. Cars left in the parking area after 10:00 PM will be towed. There is also a small, rocky parking area on

Wasatch Boulevard, which accesses the section where dogs are prohibited.

Nestled at the base of Little Cottonwood Canyon, Quail Hollow Park is a nature reprieve where you can roam through two dramatically different landscapes. In the park's northern section, big sage and rabbitbrush fields line the flat dirt trails. Trails in the southern (no dog) zone of the park straddle Little Cottonwood Creek and travel through a waterside wildlife habitat shaded by mature bigtooth maples, box elders, curl-leaf mountain mahogany, chokecherries, and cottonwoods.

Easy neighborhood access, limited elevation gain, and a mountain bike park make this a popular, mellow outing. However, there is little to no shade in the northern part of the park, so avoid this segment on scorching days.

On snowy or icy days, micro-traction spikes and hiking poles are helpful, especially near the creek. As the snow melts, be prepared for muddy conditions.

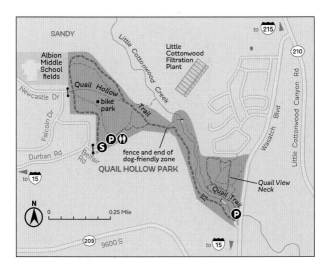

GET MOVING

Locate the parking area entrance gate in the southwest corner of the lot and begin on a narrow footpath that goes north. The flat dirt trail skirts the perimeter of peaceful homes, surrounded by open fields of native shrubs.

Arrive at a five-way intersection in about 0.3 mile. Go straight and pass the playing fields of Albion Middle School to the left. When the trail forks at 0.5 mile, go left, and after a few hundred feet, reach the lowest elevation point at 4950 feet. Skirt the perimeter of the park and witness the Wasatch peaks crowning the skyline: Mount Olympus (Hike 20) to the northeast and the Broads Fork Twin Peaks to the southeast, with a view into Bells Canyon (Hike 28) and the entrance to Little Cottonwood Canyon (Hikes 33–36).

At 0.9 mile, go left when the passage joins a double-track dirt road, Quail Hollow Trail. Ignore the numerous side trails over the next 0.1 mile and continue straight on the well-defined main path.

Veer left at a fork at 1 mile, and then travel parallel to a chain-link fence for 0.1 mile. Dogs are prohibited past the chainlink fence, so to continue exploring, leave your furry pals at home.

Mature Gambel oaks hug the trail as it narrows and becomes rockier. When the trail forks just before 1.1 miles, go right. Soon an opening reveals Little Cottonwood Creek below and the Go Farther routes on the opposite side of the water.

Stroll above the gently flowing creek and take a moment to listen for bird calls and animal sounds. Cross a bridge at 1.4 miles and begin a short, gentle ascent. Shortly past the bridge, follow a directional sign to stay on Quail Hollow Trail. A small concrete dam and Little Cottonwood Creek is visible below. Beyond the water catch, the free-flowing stream is a soothing rumble.

At 1.5 miles, Quail Hollow Trail passes next to an old metal footbridge that crosses Little Cottonwood Creek. After a few paces, end at a dirt parking lot on Wasatch Boulevard at the

The base of Little Cottonwood Canyon seen from the Quail Trail

elevation high point (5090 feet). Head back the same way or cross the metal bridge for another mile or so of exploring (see Go Farther).

To shorten the hike by 0.5 mile, when the Quail Hollow Trail intersects the gravel road at the north end of the park, turn left on the gravel road and follow it back to the trailhead. Or retrace the route you took in for a 3-mile adventure.

GO FARTHER

Cross Little Cottonwood Creek on the metal bridge. Turn left on a gravel road and stroll past the water catch. After 0.1 mile, take the narrow path to the right to begin the rocky, 300-foot ascent of the Quail Trail.

A plethora of paths explore the grassy, shrubby fields. To walk a 1-mile, counterclockwise loop with around 300 feet of elevation gain, go left at the first fork and then veer left again after a few hundred feet. Turn right on Quail View Neck and then veer right again. The trail opens to a meadow with astonishing views of the mouth of Little Cottonwood Canyon to the west.

Next, go straight through a four-way intersection as the trail hugs the border of several new homes. Continue to trend right past several forks until the path descends back to the wide dirt road. When you're ready, head back to the trailhead.

26 Dimple Dell West

DISTANCE:	3.9 miles
ELEVATION GAIN:	260 feet
HIGH POINT:	4650 feet
DIFFICULTY:	Easy to moderate
TIME:	2 hours
FITNESS:	Walkers, hikers, runners
FAMILY-FRIENDLY:	Yes
DOG-FRIENDLY:	Yes, on-leash. Waste bins at Lone Peak Park, Wrangler trailhead, and Sandy City Dog Park.
AMENITIES:	Parking, restrooms, sports courts, playgrounds, picnic tables, pavilion, trail signs
CONTACT/MAP:	Salt Lake County Parks and Open Space
GPS:	40.56746°N, 111.87633°W
BEFORE YOU GO:	Popular with mountain bikers and equestrians. Dappled shade and a mellow grade make this an excellent year-round trail.

GETTING THERE

Public Transit: Take TRAX Blue Line to the Sandy Civic Center Station. Travel south on the Porter Rockwell Trail (Hike 38). At the Sandy City Dog Park, turn left and walk toward a parking

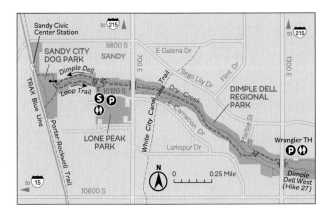

lot. Go right and look for a gate marking the entrance to Dimple Dell Park. **Bike Route:** Use the Salt Lake City & County Bikeways Map to plot a route to the trailhead. **Driving:** From I-15, take exit 295 for UT 209 / 9000 S, and go east on 9000 S for 1.5 miles. Turn right on 700 E for 1.4 miles. Turn right on 10120 S, take the first exit at the roundabout, and turn left into the parking lot on the west side of Lone Peak Park.

With more than 15 miles of trails, Dimple Dell Regional Park is a playground for hikers, bikers, and equestrians. The impressive 630-acre expanse of wilderness is nestled in the heart of the Sandy suburbs, and the proximity to the TRAX line makes it a fantastic choice for those who rely on public transportation or are looking to cut down on carbon emissions. The eastern and western parts of the park are biologically distinguished and possess a distinct character.

The west loop of Dimple Dell traverses a small valley next to a seasonal stream, aptly named Dry Creek. Portions of the hike are well-shaded under a canopy of deciduous trees, and despite bustling urban centers surrounding the natural space, the area is quiet and peaceful. Enjoy a calming stroll on a wide, mostly even woodchip path.

GET MOVING

From Lone Peak Park's northwest parking lot, go north and cross 10120 S to the overflow dirt parking area. The trail starts on a woodchip access road in the northeast corner of the lot. Look for a metal gate leading to a short descent. When you reach a T intersection, go left on the woodchip Dimple Dell Loop Trail.

The trail forks at 0.1 mile; go straight to cross a beautiful metal-and-wood bridge. Turn left after the bridge and proceed under the shade of mature Fremont cottonwood, willow, balsam poplar, chokecherry, Gambel oak, Siberian elm (invasive), and Russian olive (invasive) trees.

Encounter a T intersection at 0.4 mile and go left (right goes to the TRAX station and Sandy City Dog Park). Almost immediately, go left again to traverse Dry Creek. At 0.5 mile, arrive at the lowest elevation point, 4460 feet. Ignore the undeveloped side trails and stick to the wide, woodchip main path.

Complete a small loop at 0.7 mile when you return to the bridge. Go left to cross the bridge for a second time and then go right on the woodchip Dimple Dell Trail. At 0.8 mile, cross another bridge and then go left at a T intersection. Follow an underpass to walk beneath 700 E at 1 mile. A symphony of bird calls ring through the dense forest in this section; pull out your binoculars and guidebook if you have them.

At 1.1 miles, the course merges with an access trail; go left. Look up to see the White City Canal Trail (Hike 37, Go Farther) pedestrian bridge. Walk through a beautiful picture-frame view of Wasatch summits and cliffs, with Lone Peak to the south and Bells Canyon (Hike 28) to the north.

After the White City Canal Trail, the trees become sparser. Fragrant sumac, big sage, white sage, and saltbush team up with grasses to paint the landscape shades of jade during the spring and early summer.

A jogger crosses a bridge on the Dimple Dell Loop Trail.

Encounter a three-way fork at 1.6 miles and continue straight to stay on the woodchips. At 1.9 miles, keep left to avoid exiting the park on a paved path. After a few hundred feet, go left at the next fork. Cross a third bridge at 2 miles and keep right. Enter a dense deciduous forest and begin a short climb to a pedestrian tunnel under 1300 E.

Proceed through the tunnel (elevation 4650 feet), which marks 2.3 miles and the turnaround point. Look for the Wrangler trailhead (Hike 27) up a short path to the left.

To return to the trailhead, retrace your steps and at 3.7 miles, when the trail forks just before the second bridge, go left. After a few hundred feet, go left again to exit the park and complete the 3.9-mile sojourn.

GO FARTHER

One of the best parts about visiting the west part of Dimple Dell is its proximity to a TRAX station. Plan a full-day urban adventure sans driving. Take the TRAX to the park and link the Dimple Dell West and Dimple Dell East trails for a 10-mile quest.

27 Dimple Dell East

DISTANCE:	6-mile loop
ELEVATION GAIN:	650 feet
HIGH POINT:	5120 feet
DIFFICULTY:	Moderate
TIME:	3 hours
FITNESS:	Walkers, hikers, runners
FAMILY-FRIENDLY:	Yes
DOG-FRIENDLY:	Yes, on-leash. Waste bins at Wrangler trailhead, Mount Jordan trailhead, and Granite Park.
AMENITIES:	Parking, restrooms, trail signs, plus water at Wrangler trailhead
CONTACT/MAP:	Salt Lake County Parks and Open Space
GPS:	40.56224°N, 111.85136°W
BEFORE YOU GO:	Popular with mountain bikers and equestrians. There isn't much shade on the eastern Dimple Dell trails. A good cold-weather route.

GETTING THERE

Public Transit: Using public transit adds about 0.9 mile of walking to the route, much of it on a dirt pedestrian trail. Take UTA bus route F94 to 9800 S / 2143 E. Go west on 9800 S for just over 0.1 mile. Look for a dirt path on the left just past Falcon Hurst Drive. Follow it for 0.75 mile until it intersects with Dimple Dell Trail and turn left to begin the route. **Bike Route:** Use the Salt Lake City & County Bikeways Map to plot a route to the trailhead. **Driving:** From I-15, take exit 293 for UT 151 / 10600 S. Go east on 10600 S for 2.4 miles and then turn left on 1300 E. After 0.3 mile, look for the access road to Wrangler trailhead on the right.

Dimple Dell Regional Park, a treasured open space within the heart of suburbia, has been populated by humans for millennia. In 2015, a team of archaeologists uncovered an ancient pit house and inside found a fire pit and spearheads estimated to be 1500 years old. The archaeological site is now covered to protect the space from vandalism and looters.

The eastern side of Dimple Dell Regional Park is an excellent choice for cooler days; it features plentiful native shrubs, grasses, and flowers—but not so many shade trees. The first several miles follow Dimple Dell Trail—a flat, wide, woodchip path—and the up-close views of the Wasatch as you head east are a hiking highlight. Folks looking for an easier route can use Dimple Dell Trail as an out-and-back; the path gradually gains 450 feet of elevation over 2.75 miles. Turn around at the first Primrose Loop Trail junction for a 1.2-mile ramble, at the second Primrose Loop Trail junction for a 2.2-mile stroll, or at the first Connector Trail junction for a hike just shy of 4 miles.

GET MOVING

Start at the Wrangler trailhead, the lowest elevation point at 4690 feet. Go east and begin on Dimple Dell Trail, an easily

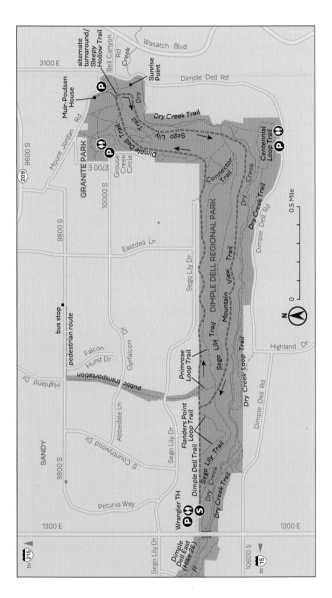

distinguished, wide, woodchip path. In the spring and early summer, fields of rye, bitterbrush, white sage, big sage, and golden currant paint the landscape in shades of green. Keep an eye out for tufted evening primrose and Utah's state flower, the sego lily.

Encounter the Flanders Point Loop Trail at 0.3 mile and go straight. At 0.6 mile, when the Flanders Point Loop Trail again merges with the Dimple Dell Trail, continue straight. After a few hundred feet, meet the Primrose Loop Trail and go straight. The path intersects the pedestrian trail for public transit users at 0.7 mile.

Over the next mile, the walkway meets numerous side paths; keep to the wide woodchip lane to stay on Dimple Dell Trail. Sensational views of Lone Peak, Bells Canyon (Hike 28), Ferguson Canyon (Hike 24), and Mount Olympus (Hike 20) make walking this section an aesthetic delight.

Around 2.4 miles, the trail network becomes denser; keep following the woodchips to stay on the main path. Reach the Sleepy Hollow Trail sign and a five-way intersection at 2.75 miles and the highest point of elevation (5120 feet). (This is also a perfect turnaround spot for a more leisurely 5.5-mile hike option).

Are you interested in history? Before beginning the next leg of the loop, check out the historic Muir-Poulsen House, which is only 0.1 mile from this junction (see Go Further).

To continue the loop, from the signed intersection, take the wide middle path that descends directly to the drainage. Walk down the steep, sandy path, keeping to the well-worn trail. At 3 miles, reach a valley basin and seasonally flowing Dry Creek—a lovely place to relax on warm days. Shortly after the trail reaches Dry Creek, it becomes a wide, woodchip path.

Veer left and stick to the broadest path as you pass three side trails over the next 0.2 mile. Go left at 3.6 miles when the Connector Trail appears to your right.

The southern portion of Dimple Dell East has a myriad of trails. Don't be overconcerned about taking a wrong turn and winding up on a different track. Continue to travel west, and enjoy the views of the Oquirrh Mountains, Kennecott Copper Mine, and Blackridge (Hike 42). The way will eventually lead back to Wrangler trailhead or the underpass just below and within sight of the trailhead.

Hiker and pup walk toward the mouth of Little Cottonwood Canyon and Bells Canyon.

GO FARTHER

Visit the 125-year-old Muir-Poulsen House, which housed James and Janet Muir from 1897 to 1938; it was repossessed during the Great Depression. Eventually, George and Alta Poulsen resettled on the property in 1942, and it still had residents up until 2015. Now the site is managed by Salt Lake County in collaboration with the Utah State Historic Preservation Office and Dimple Dell Preservation Community. Salt Lake County's master plan reveals big ambitions to restore the original homestead. In the coming years, expect a refurbished farmhouse, historical barn, orchards, outdoor classrooms, ornamental gardens, restrooms, and interpretive trails.

To find the Muir-Poulsen House, start at the signed five-way junction 2.75 miles into the hike and continue straight for 0.1 mile to reach the Mount Jordan trailhead and parking area. The Muir-Poulsen House is visible several hundred feet ahead to the left of the parking lot. Anticipate the site to change during the restoration of the homestead.

28 Bells Canyon

DISTANCE:	4.9 miles
ELEVATION GAIN:	1480 feet
HIGH POINT:	6730 feet
DIFFICULTY:	Challenging
TIME:	4 hours
FITNESS:	Hikers
FAMILY-FRIENDLY:	This is a challenging hike, but there is a 0.2-mile, ADA-accessible paved loop around Bells Canyon Preservation trailhead, perfect for strollers.
DOG-FRIENDLY:	No, dogs are prohibited.
AMENITIES:	Parking, restrooms, drinking water, waste bins, maps, interpretive signs, pavilion, picnic tables, benches, bike rack, waterfall, reservoir, fishing

CONTACT/MAP:	US Forest Service; Sandy City Parks and Recreation
GPS:	40.57143°N, 111.79810°W
BEFORE YOU GO:	Bells Canyon is a watershed, so dogs, horses, wading, swimming, and camping are prohibited. Park hours are from dawn to 10:00 PM. Rattlesnake sightings are common. Prime wildflower months are June to August. Gorgeous fall colors. For winter travel, avalanche education and equipment are recommended.

GETTING THERE

Public Transit: Taking public transit adds 1.5 miles of walking; a bike makes the commute easier. Take UTA bus route F94 and get off at Mount Jordan Road / 9658 S. Go north for a few hundred feet, turn right on UT 209 / 9600 S, and travel for 1.2 miles. At Wasatch Boulevard, look for the enormous Bells Canyon Preservation trailhead diagonally across the intersection. Follow the footpath to the top parking tier and trailhead. **Bike Route:** Use the Salt Lake City & County Bikeways Map to plot a route to the trailhead. **Driving:** From I-15, take exit 295 for UT 209 / 9000 S and go east for 4.8 miles. Turn right on Mount Jordan Road and drive for 0.8 mile. Turn right on Dimple Dell Road, followed by an immediate left onto Bell Canyon Road. Go left on Wasatch Boulevard for 0.2 mile and find the Bell Canyon Preservation trailhead on the right.

It's easy to understand why Bells Canyon is enormously popular: on this hike you'll be rewarded with impressive peak views, flowing water, quiet reflection spots around a placid reservoir, and a jaw-dropping cascade thundering over granite cliffs. In 2022, the City of Sandy constructed the Bell Canyon Preservation trailhead to help with the increasing foot traffic—it features a paved pedestrian loop, 133 parking spaces, year-round restrooms, picnic sites, and educational resources.

Lower Bell Canyon Dam, with its reflective reservoir, is just over half a mile from the preservation trailhead. There is not one iota of shade until after the reservoir. The lower section can

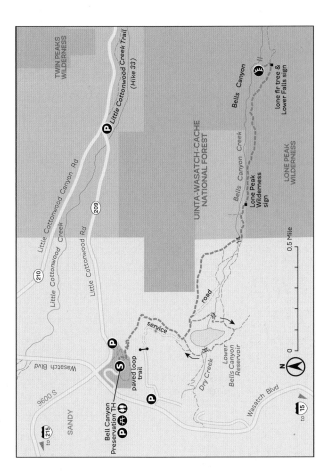

be brutally hot during the summer, so start early, and bring a lot of water. Poles are helpful year-round. During the winter, hiking to the reservoir is a good option, and micro-traction spikes or snowshoes are recommended.

There are too many unofficial side trails and shortcuts to note them all. Stay on the well-worn main path, avoid shortcuts, and don't bushwhack.

GET MOVING

There are three trailheads. This out-and-back route starts from Bell Canyon Preservation trailhead's upper parking lot (elevation 5250 feet). The "Protected Watershed Area" sign a few feet north of the restrooms marks the start on the gravel double track. After a few hundred feet, the way forks. Go left (right accesses the paved loop trail). Then in a few feet, go right (left goes toward the trailhead on 9600 S).

The trail quickly narrows, becoming dirt and rock. Avoid shortcuts as you complete a series of switchbacks. When the grade backs off, take a breather and admire the splashes of color from heat-loving plants like Gambel oak, big sagebrush, white sage, goldenrod, and arrowleaf balsamroot.

After 350 feet of elevation gain, the track forks at 0.6 mile on the north end of the Lower Bell Canyon Reservoir. Go left at the fork and ascend a dirt double track for 0.1 mile. Come to another fork and veer left (right loops around the reservoir, the Go Farther route). Look for the "waterfall 1.2 miles" wood sign at 0.75 mile and turn left off the double track onto a narrow dirt trail. Soon after, the path opens to a small meadow and a sensational view up Bells Canyon.

After the meadow, watch for mile marker signs every quarter mile. The biodiversity begins to intensify—mature white firs, bigtooth maples, curl-leaf mountain mahogany, and chokecherry trees provide welcome shade on hot days and paint the mountain in warm motifs come autumn.

The trail forks near the creek just after the 1.25 mile marker sign. Go left and cross a wood footbridge. The bridge marks just shy of 600 feet of elevation gain from the trailhead, which leaves almost 900 feet of elevation gain for the final mile or so.

Go left after the bridge and then keep left to stay on the main track. The ascent becomes steeper, rockier, and more challenging. Dappled shade and clusters of tufted fleabane,

Opposite: *Bells Canyon's magnificent waterfall cascades over white granite.*

sego lily, sticky purple geranium, silky lupine, and whorled buckwheat liven the climb with color.

Keep right to avoid a deceiving side path at 1.5 miles and pass the "Lone Peak Wilderness" sign at 1.6 miles. After the wilderness sign, the trail moves near the running water of Bells Canyon Creek, which creates a soothing melody accompanied by the rustling leaves of aspen and box elder trees. Full shade and running water make this a lovely area to stop for a refresher before the final grind to the waterfall.

The final half mile before the falls is the steepest, but there are several places to take a breather and gaze at the immense cliffs to the north. Finally, at 2.4 miles, the steep trail comes to the waterfall turn-off point, which can be easy to miss during the grueling ascent. There are two helpful markers: an enormous lone fir tree amid an aspen forest and (hopefully) a wood plank with a hand-drawn arrow and the words "Lower Falls" scrawled in marker.

This waterfall turn-off point is the highest point of elevation at 6730 feet. Go left toward the falls and follow the easiest path for several hundred feet toward the rumble. Your first sight of the cascade will make the strenuous climb worth every step. The roar and mist of the tumbling water reward you with a cleansing and mesmerizing experience. Rocky Mountain juniper and yellow columbines color the shadows while zipping birds and floating butterflies dance to the rhythm of the mountain-water cascade.

After ample rest and sensory rejuvenation, reverse your steps to the trailhead to complete the 4.9-mile adventure.

GO FARTHER

The loop around Lower Bells Canyon Reservoir adds 0.75 mile and just under 100 feet of elevation gain. From the double track near the north end of the reservoir, take the narrow dirt trail to the south and immediately enter a shady tree canopy.

After a few feet, go left at the first fork. At the next junction, an aesthetic wooden footbridge is visible to the right; cross the bridge and then turn left. Veer right at the next three forks as the path moves out of the shady forest. Then at 0.6 mile, come to a large wooden bridge—this is a popular place to soak up the views. Go right after the bridge and follow the double track as it ascends. Swerve right just before intersecting the approach trail to complete the 0.75-mile loop.

Next page: *Scarlet skyrocket, arrowleaf balsamroot, and buckwheat meadows below Sundial Peak (Hike 29)*

BIG COTTONWOOD CANYON

The curving road of Big Cottonwood Canyon with its flowing creek, dense vegetation, and dramatic summits is overwhelmingly beautiful. For a unique way to experience the canyon, take the self-guided Big Cottonwood Canyon Geology Tour, which starts at the Big Cottonwood Canyon Park and Ride and stops at geologically interesting pullouts throughout the canyon. Informational plaques point out and describe fossil remains, 700-million-year-old rocks, and mud and sand deposited from ancient seas.

The quartzite spires, cliffs, and peaks that rise sharply from the winding canyon floor provide countless rock-climbing possibilities. Toward the top of the canyon are two of Salt Lake's infamous ski resorts, Brighton and Solitude. Within the canyon, numerous campgrounds and picnic areas perfectly complement hikes. The four routes featured in this section range from mellow wanders to rigorous outings.

Big Cottonwood Canyon is part of the Salt Lake watershed, so dogs and horses are never permitted and swimming in the lakes is prohibited. During winter, hiking areas may be inaccessible, and avalanche safety education and equipment are recommended. There is no public transportation outside of ski season.

29 Lake Blanche

DISTANCE:	6.2 miles
ELEVATION GAIN:	2670 feet
HIGH POINT:	8880 feet
DIFFICULTY:	Challenging
TIME:	4.5 hours
FITNESS:	Hikers
FAMILY-FRIENDLY:	It's a steep hike and may be challenging for young children. But from the trailhead, a 0.6-mile out-and-back paved path next to the river is suitable for strollers and ADA-accessible.
DOG-FRIENDLY:	No, dogs are prohibited.
AMENITIES:	Parking, restrooms, trail information, picnic area, backcountry camping
CONTACT/MAP:	US Forest Service
GPS:	40.63338°N, 111.72353°W
BEFORE YOU GO:	Be prepared for weekend crowds. Lake Blanche is part of Salt Lake City's watershed: no swimming or dogs. Prime wildflower months are June through August. Beautiful fall foliage. For winter travel, avalanche education and equipment are recommended.

GETTING THERE

Driving: From I-215, take exit 6 for 6200 S and go southeast for 1.9 miles. Turn left on UT 190 E/Big Cottonwood Canyon Road. Follow UT 190 E up a winding road for 4.3 miles to the Mill B South Fork trailhead at the bottom of the S curve. Turn right into the parking lot.

Hike out to Lake Blanche and find a feast for the eyes: a stunning alpine lake surrounded by craggy Wasatch peaks. It's a popular destination hike, and with good reason. The rich deciduous forest paints the landscape in warm colors come autumn, and the well-defined trail, diverse foliage, and changing vistas make for an enjoyable climb. With almost 3000

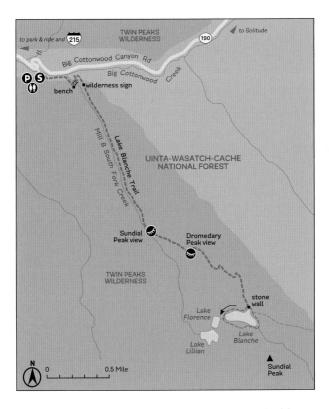

feet of elevation gain in just over 3 miles, it's also a legitimate workout.

Even though the lowest point of elevation is over 6000 feet, sections of this hike have no shade, and it can be hot. During the summer months, start early and bring plenty of water. For winter travel, snowshoes or micro-traction spikes and poles are recommended.

GET MOVING

Locate the restrooms and the information kiosk in the southeast corner of the parking area. The trailhead is near the

View of Sundial Peak from the shores of Lake Blanche

restrooms and is the lowest point of elevation at 6200 feet. Begin on a paved pedestrian path parallel to Big Cottonwood Creek. Pass the Lake Blanche map and look for a steep, rocky trail to the right at about 0.2 mile. Turn onto the Lake Blanche Trail and begin the ascent.

Follow the well-shaded trail under a canopy of balsam poplar, box elder, and white fir trees. At 0.4 mile, arrive at a commemorative bench and a wood footbridge. Cross Mill B South Fork Creek on the bridge and then go left, following the trail sign.

The trail immediately begins scaling west-facing terrain; the next 0.8 mile is primarily exposed, only occasionally dipping into the shade. Heat-loving shrubs like Gambel oak, big sage, and white sage flourish here.

Pass the "Twin Peaks Wilderness" sign at 0.5 mile. In sections where the trail moves close to the creek, thimbleberry, red raspberry, and spreading dogbane thrive among scattered Rocky Mountain junipers.

The first quaking aspen grove appears at about 1.2 miles. For the next 0.8 mile, meander under the dappled shade of increasingly mature aspens and bigtooth maples, as aspen fleabanes, nettleleaf horsemint, showy goldeneyes, and multiple aster species paint the understory in gold and purple.

After 1400 feet of climbing, at 2 miles, the tip of Sundial Peak comes into view. Enjoy the scenic landscape and a brief respite as the grade backs off for 0.25 mile, rambling through dense aspens to a vista of Dromedary Peak. Keep pushing on as the incline gets steeper, rockier, and more exposed—you have about 800 feet of elevation left to gain in less than 1 mile.

To make the climb more enjoyable, look for whorled buckwheat, coyote mint, and sulphur-flower buckwheat among the quartzite boulders. Meadows of arrowleaf balsamroot and a "Help Protect Your Watershed" sign mark a few hundred feet below the top.

At 3.1 miles, the trail ends at a stone wall and the highest point of elevation, 8880 feet. Walk a few feet down toward the shore of Lake Blanche and find a spot to enjoy the views. Look for Monte Cristo Peak to the southeast, the Broads Fork Twin Peaks to the southwest, and the up-close perspective of the closest peak, Sundial (keep an eye out for rock climbers on Sundial, a popular climbing objective). It's a great spot for a picnic—but resist feeding the cute Uinta ground squirrels. Giving them human food is a big disservice. Instead, see if you can snap a photo of one munching on paintbrush.

Want to do a bit more exploring? Take the 0.9-mile walk around the lake (see Go Farther). Otherwise, retrace the trail to return to the trailhead and complete your 6.2-mile excursion.

GO FARTHER

The lake loop is simply gorgeous, traversing through fields of wildflowers and gaining a 360-degree perspective of Lake Blanche. A few steep climbs gain and lose about 100 feet of elevation.

To start the counterclockwise loop, follow the trail toward the lake from the stone wall, and go right. Veer left to stay on the trail as it hugs the lake and clambers over rocks. After 0.3 mile, the path moves through a break in the stone wall. Then it steeply climbs to the opposite side; traverse the remains of the stone wall for several hundred feet.

About halfway around the lake, at 8970 feet elevation, enjoy the wildflower foreground and the immense Sundial Peak backdrop before two creek crossings. Return to the stone wall at the end of your 0.9-mile lakeside saunter.

30 Donut Falls

DISTANCE:	3.6 miles
ELEVATION GAIN:	500 feet
HIGH POINT:	7740 feet
DIFFICULTY:	Easy to moderate
TIME:	3 hours
FITNESS:	Hikers, runners
FAMILY-FRIENDLY:	Yes, a popular hike for children and adults of all ages.
DOG-FRIENDLY:	No, dogs are prohibited.
AMENITIES:	Parking, restrooms, trail signs, waterfall, campground

CONTACT/MAP:	US Forest Service
GPS:	40.64965°N, 111.64890°W
BEFORE YOU GO:	Be prepared for crowds, especially on weekends and holidays. A very short (10 feet or so) downclimb right before the waterfall can feel challenging. Walking in shallow (1- to 2-inch deep) water is necessary to gain a view of the falls; be prepared to have wet feet or bring water shoes. For winter travel, avalanche education and equipment are recommended.

GETTING THERE

Driving: From I-215, take exit 6 for 6200 S and go southeast for 1.9 miles. Turn left on UT 190 E / Big Cottonwood Canyon Road, and drive for 9 miles. Look for a large parking area on the right, across the highway from Mill D North Fork trailhead. An alternate trailhead bypasses the first half of the hike, 0.8 mile south on S. Cardiff Fork Road. However, the lower portion of the walk is lovely, and parking at the alternate trailhead is limited.

Donut Falls boasts seasonal highlights year-round, and it's no wonder that it is one of the most popular hikes in the Salt Lake region. Splashes of bright color from countless shrubs and wildflowers line the trail during the blooming months. Burnt orange and gold shade the scape in autumn, and winter is a dazzling snowy scene crisscrossed by snowshoers. And of course, at the end of the short, well-trodden trail, a stellar waterfall awaits.

The well-signed path is easy to follow, with a gentle grade and a lot of shade. Poles are helpful for navigating the short river section. During snowy months, snowshoes or micro-traction spikes are recommended.

GET MOVING

The Mill D North Fork trailhead marks the lowest elevation at 7270 feet. Locate the newly constructed boardwalk a few

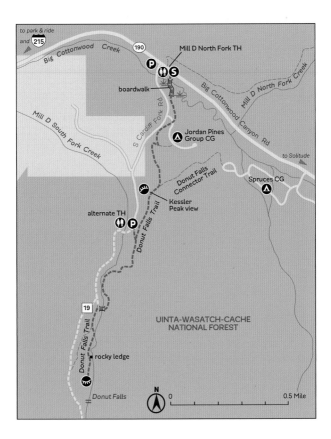

paces up-canyon from the restrooms. Follow the boardwalk across the wetlands to intercept the Donut Falls Trail at 0.2 mile and turn left on the wide, worn, dirt passage with very few rocks. Hike through a field of big sage, whorled buckwheat, Wasatch beardtongue, and Jacob's-ladders. Encounter a road with a signed junction at 0.3 mile, and continue straight toward Donut Falls.

The shrubs transition to mature white firs, Douglas firs, and scattered stands of quaking aspen around 0.3 mile. The

A family enjoys the mellow climb to Donut Falls through an aspen forest.

rest of the trek is mainly shaded and gently climbs in a heavily coniferous forest filled with dozens of wildflower species. Stands of Rocky Mountain blue columbine take center stage among fringed bluebells, heartleaf arnica, elkweed, sticky purple geraniums, Richardson's geranium, Pacific ninebark, and Woods' rose.

Meet a signed junction at 0.4 mile, veer right to follow the arrow, and continue toward Donut Falls (left goes toward Jordan Pines Group Campground, see Go Further). When the forest opens at 0.6 mile, Kesler Peak dominates the skyline to the southwest. The trail forks a few feet after the Kesler Peak view; go right (left goes toward Spruces Campground, see Go Further).

Around 1 mile, after gaining about 200 feet of elevation, come to the upper trailhead, which intersects the main path near some restrooms. From here, the trail gets a bit steeper and rockier. Shortly after the alternate trailhead, listen for Mill D South Fork Creek gurgling in the drainage to the right. Cross the stream on a small wood footbridge at 1.4 miles.

After the bridge, go left on a gravel double track and then at 1.5 miles, go left at a fork. Encounter the "Salt Lake City Watershed Area" sign at 1.7 miles, immediately before a short downclimb. A fixed line aids in the descent of the 10- to 15-foot rocky ledge. After the descent, head up the stream, wading in the shallow flow.

Follow the water for 0.1 mile to obtain the highest point of elevation (7740 feet) and a view of the falls. To the right of the waterfall, a rock face (often wet and slippery) offers a Class 3 scramble. The view before the scramble is sensational, however, so this hike description ends here.

Find a spot to gaze at the falls. Enjoy witnessing the frolicking families before retracing the route to the trailhead to complete the 3.6-mile sojourn.

GO FURTHER

After a beautiful hike, nothing beats returning to camp to kick back and enjoy a reprieve from city life. There are two family-friendly campgrounds with hiking trails that intercept the Donut Falls Trail. Spruces Campground features modern amenities and more than one hundred campsites. Jordan Pines Group Campground is for large groups (fifty or more people). Contact the USFS Salt Lake Ranger District to make a reservation.

31 Willow Lake Heights

DISTANCE:	2.6-mile loop
ELEVATION GAIN:	640 feet
HIGH POINT:	8540 feet
DIFFICULTY:	Moderate
TIME:	2 hours
FITNESS:	Hikers, runners
FAMILY-FRIENDLY:	Yes
DOG-FRIENDLY:	No, dogs are prohibited.
AMENITIES:	Roadside parking; the closest restrooms are at Solitude Mountain Resort
CONTACT/MAP:	US Forest Service
GPS:	40.63022˚N, 111.60464˚W
BEFORE YOU GO:	Prime wildflower months are July and August. Stunning fall colors. The north end of the lake loop moves through avalanche terrain. In winter, avalanche education and equipment are recommended.

GETTING THERE

Public Transit: Available only during ski season. Take UTA Ski Bus route 972 to Silver Fork Lodge. Walk down Big Cottonwood Canyon Road and take the first right, immediately followed by a right onto Mountain Sun Lane. Stay on Mountain Sun Lane, passing two forks, and then at a four-way intersection, go straight. The road becomes Willow Heights Trail 0.4 mile from the bus stop. Travel on Willow Heights Trail for 0.1 mile until the path encounters the main trail. **Driving:** From I-215, take exit 6 for 6200 S and go southeast for 1.9 miles. Turn left

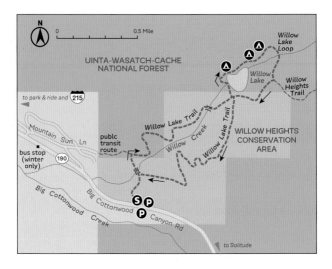

on UT 190 E / Big Cottonwood Canyon Road. Follow UT 190 E up a winding road for 11.5 miles. At 9.5 miles, pass Spruces Campground. After 2 more miles, look for a granite marker for Willow Heights Conservation Area on the left. There is no designated parking lot; park on the roadside. During ski season, expect heavy weekend traffic and limited parking.

Meander on the Willow Lake Trail through a continuous aspen forest, which becomes a blaze of gold and strawberry-blond leaves in autumn. Wildflowers weave a tapestry of colors in the open meadows near the lake in the spring and summer. With all this natural beauty, it's alarming to think the 155-acre Willow Heights Conservation Area was once on the verge of development, nearly becoming rows of condos and vacation homes. Luckily for nature lovers, Utah Open Lands partnered with Salt Lake City and the Utah Quality Growth Commission to successfully preserve the area in 2001.

Moose, elk, and deer sightings are common in the conservation area; be respectful of wildlife by keeping your distance and not creating a racket. On snowy or icy days, snowshoes or micro-traction spikes and poles are helpful.

GET MOVING

A commemorative engraving on a large granite boulder marks the Willow Heights Conservation Area trailhead on the north side of Big Cottonwood Canyon Road. The well-worn, single-track path starts at the lowest point of elevation, 7900 feet.

Begin on the continuously ascending trail through dense quaking aspens. When you reach an intersection at just over 0.1 mile, go left and cross Willow Creek on a small footbridge. Come to a signed junction at 0.2 mile, where the path encounters the alternative approach from the bus stop. Go right and follow the main trail as it climbs a gully.

Prime months for golden aspens at Willow Lake are September and October.

Clamber through the quaking aspens as the traffic sounds diminish with each step. At 0.5 mile and 8230 feet elevation, scatterings of Scots pines appear. The pine and aspen branches wrap around each other, and during autumn, a golden confetti of aspen leaves float among the pine needles.

Cross a second bridge at 0.8 mile (elevation 8430 feet). The approach opens to a meadow brimming with big sage, asters, aspen fleabane, showy goldeneye, and silky lupine. Meander through the field for 0.1 mile to a junction below Willow Lake.

Go left at the junction and immediately veer left again to begin the 0.6-mile clockwise loop around Willow Lake. Ignore the numerous side trails; stick to the well-worn main path and don't bushwhack. If the track peters out, turn around to regain the main trail.

Plan for time to bask in the quiet forest and take in the nourishing views surrounding the lake loop. Several perfect picnic places line the north side of the lake, along with a few backcountry camping spots. At 1.2 miles, just past the last backcountry camp area, attain the hike's highest elevation at 8540 feet. On the east part of the lake loop, veer right when the trail forks at 1.4 miles. Continue for another 0.2 mile to complete the loop.

At the four-way junction after the lake loop, go left to begin a descent (straight is the approach trail). Mount Wolverine, Patsy Marley Peak, and Honeycomb Cliffs crown the southern skyline. An opening in the aspens at 2.1 miles reveals Mount Raymond and Wildcat Ridge to the west. Continue down beneath the canopy of aspens for another 0.4 mile before arriving at a familiar fork and bridge. Go left and retrace your steps to the trailhead to complete the hike.

GO FURTHER

One of two accredited land trusts in the state, Utah Open Lands is responsible for conserving the land around Willow Lake. Land trusts are a precious community asset; they purchase land or development rights and work with willing landowners to create easements that preserve open spaces and permanently prevent future development.

Contribute to keeping wild places wild. Contact Utah Open Lands for volunteer or donation information (see Resources).

32 Brighton Lakes Loop

DISTANCE:	4.5-mile loop
ELEVATION GAIN:	1130 feet
HIGH POINT:	9540 feet
DIFFICULTY:	Moderate to challenging
TIME:	3 hours
FITNESS:	Walkers, hikers, runners
FAMILY-FRIENDLY:	Yes, although it may be a robust hike for young children. The boardwalk around Silver Lake (see Go Farther) is jogger stroller–friendly and ADA-accessible.
DOG-FRIENDLY:	No, dogs are prohibited.
AMENITIES:	Parking, restrooms (year-round), drinking water, visitor center, picnic tables, maps, interpretive signs
CONTACT/MAP:	US Forest Service
GPS:	40.60343°N, 111.58434°W
BEFORE YOU GO:	The lakes are part of Salt Lake City's watershed: no swimming or dogs. The Silver Lake Visitor Center is open seven days a week, May through September. Stop in for maps, activities, and hiking tips. Prime wildflower months are July and August. Much of the route is inaccessible during winter months, when the ski resort is in operation and the visitor center becomes the Solitude Nordic Center (snowshoe and Nordic ski rentals, lessons, and tours for a fee).

GETTING THERE

Public Transit: Available only during ski season. Take UTA Ski Bus route 972 to the Solitude Nordic Center. **Driving:** From I-215, take exit 6 for 6200 S and go southeast for 1.9 miles.

Turn left on UT 190 E / Big Cottonwood Canyon Road. Follow UT 190 for 14 miles. Pass Solitude Mountain Resort at 12 miles. Look for the Silver Lake Visitor Center and parking on the right, across the road from Brighton Store and Cafe.

Feeling hot in the Valley? The Brighton Lakes Loop hike starts at nearly 9000 feet, so it's a great choice for scorching

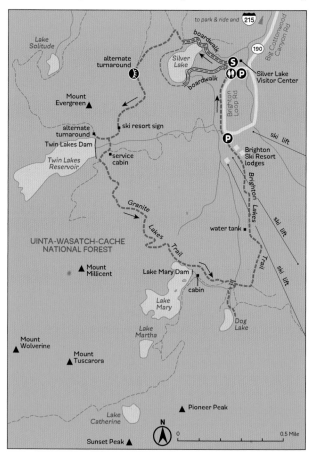

Views of Sunset Peak and Mount Tuscarora from Lake Mary

summer days. Stunning alpine lakes, quartzite spires, lush forests, and fields of wildflowers, plus a family-friendly boardwalk around Silver Lake make this area a popular destination. Wildlife thrives here—keep an eye out for moose.

This route visits four alpine lakes and reservoirs in a 4.5-mile loop. Plan extra time to explore the boardwalk, interpretive signs, and viewing docks along the 1-mile loop around Silver Lake (see Go Farther). Be aware that summer means bugs and weather can change quickly at any time of year. Bring mosquito repellant and prepare for mountain weather with extra layers and a raincoat, even when it's more than 100 degrees F in Salt Lake City. Hiking poles are helpful for steep and rocky sections.

GET MOVING

Locate the information kiosk on the paved path on the north side of the visitor center. Proceed to the right of the kiosk along the boardwalk above a marshland bursting with reeds, grasses, and sedges. Take a moment to gaze southwest across Silver Lake at the dramatic talus slopes descending from Mount Millicent's pointy summit and Mount Evergreen's fir-covered crags.

When the boardwalk turns to dirt and reaches a T inter-section, turn left. In another 0.1 mile, at a signed four-way junction, go straight on the trail toward Twin Lakes/Lake Solitude. Climb under a canopy of mature aspen. At a signed intersection, veer left toward Twin Lakes.

Gain 200 feet of elevation over the next 0.3 mile. In summer, the aspen community undergrowth is a patchwork of Woods' roses, showy goldeneyes, nettleleaf horsemint, fringed bluebells, and Wasatch beardtongues.

Reach a fork at 0.7 mile and stay left on a wide, worn, and rocky path through a talus field to a sensational view of Silver Lake and the surrounding wetlands. Since the trail beyond becomes steeper and rockier, this is an enjoyable turnaround point for a mellow, 1.5-mile round-trip.

To continue on to Twin Lakes Reservoir, ignore the many undeveloped side trails and remain on the obvious, well-worn path.

Fields of luminescent white Rocky Mountain columbine with smatterings of hot-pink splitleaf paintbrush make this rough section more enjoyable. When you reach the ski resort trail sign at 1.1 miles, your climb to Twin Lakes Reservoir is nearly complete. Shortly beyond, a double-track road intersects from the left. For now, you will head straight to the visible Twin Lakes Dam at 1.3 miles. Walk past the dam to a lovely beach with views of the top of the Milly Express ski lift, Mount Wolverine, and Patsy Marley Peak, and take a well-deserved break from your 730-foot climb. This is also an excellent turn-around point for a 2.6-mile out-and-back hike.

To continue on to Lake Mary and Dog Lake, retrace the trail to the double track, and go right for a few hundred feet. At a service cabin, go right on a short, steep ascent up a double track to a junction with the Granite Lakes Trail, where you will turn left.

Immediately the path narrows and begins a gentle descent. Over the next mile, the trail gently gains and loses elevation as it meanders through boulder gardens and forests of subalpine firs. The abundant wildflowers include a host of fleabanes, including Garrett's fleabane, a rare species endemic to the Wasatch.

Around 2.5 miles, the north rim of Lake Mary comes into sight. There are a multitude of social trails around the lake; please stay on the most well-worn path to preserve the delicate plants in this alpine environment. Look for a flat-topped lakeside boulder to use as a lounge and enjoy the regenerative beauty and silence of the lake and surrounding Pioneer Peak, Sunset Peak, and Mount Tuscarora. Plan to stay for a bit and spiritually refuel before continuing the route.

At 9540 feet, Lake Mary Dam is the highest point on the trail. Just beyond the dam, pass a cabin and reach a junction with a trail that heads to Lake Martha and Lake Catherine. To continue your loop, veer left. At the next junction, 2.7 miles from the start, go left, cross a wood footbridge, and after several paces, come to another intersection.

WASATCH WILDFLOWER FESTIVAL

The Silver Lake Visitor Center is operated by the Cottonwood Canyons Foundation, Salt Lake Ranger District, and Solitude Mountain Resort. Silver Lake is one of the stops for the annual Wasatch Wildflower Festival, which celebrates the hundreds of species of wildflowers growing in the area with free guided wildflower walks and education booths. Visit the Cottonwood Canyons Foundation website (cottonwoodcanyons.org) for information.

Garrett's fleabane, a species endemic to the Wasatch Range

Are you up for a final lake? If so, go right for a 0.4-mile roundtrip visit to pristine Dog Lake. Through a series of junctions, follow the signs to Dog Lake until the trail ends near the northeast marsh.

Take a moment to listen to Dog Lake's avian chorus of warblers, sparrows, swallows, and chickadees before retracing the trail back to the Brighton Lakes Trail, 3.2 miles from the start. Go right to begin a 1.3-mile descent back to the visitor center.

Avoid turning off the well-worn Brighton Lakes Trail on access roads and paths. Keep left when the way forks at 3.5 miles, then pass a water tank on the left. Near the resort center, when the path comes to a four-way intersection, turn right for a few steps, and then left to pass the Brighton Ski Resort lodges just before reaching the Brighton Ski Resort parking lot. Continue north through the parking lot and along Brighton Loop Road to return to the visitor center, ending your 4.5-mile adventure.

GO FARTHER

The 1-mile Silver Lake Loop circumnavigates a pristine alpine lake with a boardwalk and flat dirt paths. With ample observation decks and resting spots, it's perfect for families, picnicking, birding, and contemplation.

Start the loop on the pavement south of the visitor center. After a few hundred feet, go left on the boardwalk, passing a beautiful viewing deck before the boardwalk turns to dirt after a quarter of a mile. The dirt trail is flat, so jogger-strollers and all-terrain wheelchairs should be able to navigate the route.

Follow the path as it hugs the lake and eventually returns to the boardwalk at 0.8 mile. Use the boardwalk to complete the 1-mile loop and return to the visitor center.

Next page: *The shores of Cecret Lake (Hike 36)*

LITTLE COTTONWOOD CANYON

Devoted skiers and snowboarders refer to Little Cottonwood Canyon as "The Epicenter of the Universe." Winter here brings an abundance of snow. The Snowbird and Alta ski resorts are infamous for steep powder skiing, and the mountain town of Alta made history in 1938 when it became home to the second ski chairlift ever constructed in the United States.

Alta has a rich backstory. Founded around 1865, the town was a seasonal residence for employees of the Emma Silver Mine. The population boomed to several thousand inhabitants until 1873, when a wildfire and enormous avalanches almost eliminated human settlement. These days, Alta has fewer than 500 full-time residents, yet Little Cottonwood Canyon sees over a million visitors a year.

With its dramatic mountain beauty and abundance of opportunities for nature play, Little Cottonwood Canyon draws all types of outdoor enthusiasts. When the snow clears, hikers, runners, and mountain bikers come out to stretch their legs and spin their wheels on the numerous trails. Rock climbers love the white granite cliffs—keep an eye out for the climbing routes visible from Little Cottonwood Canyon Road. For all, the high alpine environment offers a cool escape from the city heat during sticky summer months.

Please be aware that Little Cottonwood Canyon is part of the Salt Lake City watershed, so dogs and horses are never permitted and swimming is not allowed in lakes. Trails can meander through avalanche terrain, and hiking areas may be inaccessible during the winter. For winter hiking or travel, avalanche education and equipment are recommended. Public transportation is only available during ski season.

33 Little Cottonwood Creek Trail

DISTANCE:	3.3 miles one way or 6.3 miles roundtrip
ELEVATION GAIN:	1180 feet
HIGH POINT:	6600 feet
DIFFICULTY:	Moderate
TIME:	2 hours or 4 hours
FITNESS:	Walkers, hikers, runners
FAMILY-FRIENDLY:	Yes, and the trailhead starts at the paved, ADA-accessible Temple Quarry Trail (see Go Farther)—a 0.3-mile path ideal for strollers.
DOG-FRIENDLY:	No, dogs are prohibited.
AMENITIES:	Parking, restrooms, interpretive signs, waterfall
CONTACT/MAP:	US Forest Service
GPS:	40.57191°N, 111.77470°W
BEFORE YOU GO:	The first quarter of the hike has little to no shade; the rest is well-shaded and near the creek.
	Little Cottonwood Creek is part of Salt Lake's watershed: no swimming, wading, or dogs. For winter travel, avalanche education and equipment are recommended.

GETTING THERE

Public Transit: Using public transit adds 2.5 miles of walking each way. A bike makes the commute easier. Take UTA bus route F94 and get off at Mount Jordan Road / 9658 S. Consult the Salt Lake City and County Bikeways Map. **Bike Route:** Use the Salt Lake City & County Bikeways Map to plot a route to the trailhead. **Driving:** From I-215, take exit 6 for 6200 S / UT 190 / Wasatch Boulevard and go southeast. Stay on Wasatch Boulevard for 4 miles, then go straight at the stoplight when it becomes UT 210 / Little Cottonwood Canyon Road. After 1.5 miles, turn right on Little Cottonwood Road and immediately look for the Temple Quarry gate and parking lot on the left. The gate closes seasonally during the winter. Alternate winter parking is at the Little Cottonwood Canyon Park and Ride

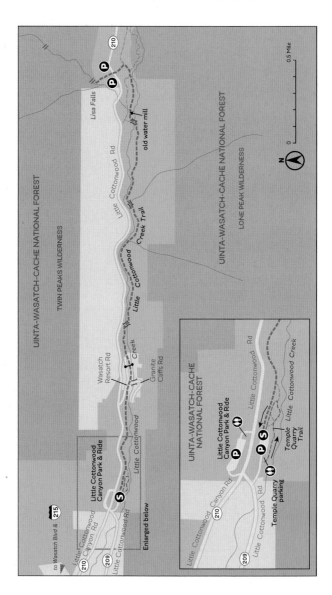

Hikers cross a shallow drainage above the old water mill.

(which is often full of skier traffic). To use a car shuttle for a shorter hike, park a car 2.7 miles farther up Little Cottonwood Road at the Lisa Falls parking area.

Wander under canopies of mature trees along Little Cottonwood Creek as the soothing crash of water drowns out any traffic noise. This trail is understandably popular year-round. The gentle, consistent grade and abundant shade on the last three-quarters of the trek appeal to hikers, joggers, and bikers alike. Lush stream-fed life hugs the trail, creating a comforting cacophony of bird calls, flowing water, and colorful plant species. A visit to Lisa Falls, a sheer cascade of water over a steep granite slab, is the cherry on top.

Late spring and summer bring gorgeous wildflower blooms, and flashy foliage debuts in the fall. The trail follows a creek, so protect yourself from bugs with long pants and long-sleeved shirts in summer. In snowy conditions, hiking poles and snowshoes or micro-traction spikes are recommended.

GET MOVING

Locate the gravel/dirt double track that begins on the eastern edge of the parking area. (The paved path parallel to the double track is the Temple Quarry Trail; see Go Farther.) Start on the most exposed section of the hike, with the best views of Little Cottonwood Canyon's infamous white granite. The imposing slabs, spires, and cliffs to the right feature classic rock-climbing objectives like *Perla's Ridge* and numerous routes on Super Slab.

Gradually ascend 200 feet in 0.7 mile as white sage, rabbitbrush, grasses, spreading fleabane, and lupine line the path. When the route intercepts Wasatch Resort Road, look for a trail sign and continue onto Granite Cliffs Road. Follow the pavement, and look for another trail sign pointing right; the pavement then becomes dirt. Cross through a gate to continue on Little Cottonwood Creek Trail.

After the gate, the course moves closer to Little Cottonwood Creek and the vegetation changes dramatically. The temperature plummets in the shade of mature box elder, Fremont cottonwood, peachleaf willow, white fir, bigtooth maple, and Gambel oak trees. The perennial creek, which sometimes rages, carves out a riparian habitat teeming with biodiversity. During the summer, the path bursts with bright-white and pastel flowers from Pacific ninebark, red-osier dogwood, thimbleberry, raspberry, and Woods' rose. In autumn, the shrubs glow red, orange, and gold.

At 1.1 miles and 5740 feet elevation, cross the first of three bridges. Shortly after, the route encounters some impressively sized boulders. Follow the trail as it narrows and becomes rockier before crossing a second bridge at 2 miles. Soon the slender, white trunks of an aspen forest emerge. Enjoy a riverside symphony conducted by the many species of birds.

Several climbing access trails merge with the Little Cottonwood Creek Trail in this section; stay on the main, well-worn path. Cross the final bridge at 2.6 miles (elevation 6280 feet), and then keep right at the next fork. Walk past an old water mill and cross a shallow drainage (no bridge). After that, the trail gets rockier and steeper. At 2.9 miles, when the path merges with a side trail, continue straight. Reach a fork after several paces and turn left to stay on Little Cottonwood Creek Trail. Enjoy a spectacular view of Broads Fork Twin Peaks straight ahead. Then go left to reach Little Cottonwood Canyon Road and the Little Cottonwood Canyon Trail access parking area at 3 miles.

The short jaunt to Lisa Falls is 0.3 mile roundtrip and is indisputably worth the effort. Use caution when crossing Little Cottonwood Canyon Road to the Lisa Falls parking area. The Lisa Falls Trail starts at the east end of the Lisa Falls parking area.

Climb steeply, gaining over 100 feet of elevation in just over a tenth of a mile. Reach Lisa Falls, which marks the high point at 6600 feet elevation. Take a moment to gaze at the cascade of water flowing over an immense white-granite slab before following the trail down to the Lisa Falls parking area, which marks 3.3 miles from the start.

If you've planned a car shuttle, you're done for the day. Otherwise, reverse your steps back down the canyon for a 6.3-mile roundtrip excursion.

GO FARTHER

The paved, 0.3-mile Temple Quarry Trail is a biologically diverse, educational experience. To begin, locate the paved path east of the restrooms in the Temple Quarry parking area. Keep veering right when the track forks to make a counterclockwise loop. Plan for enough time to read the historical and geographical interpretive signs and lounge on one of the many benches, soaking up the mountain sights and river sounds.

34 White Pine Lake

DISTANCE:	10.4 miles
ELEVATION GAIN:	900 to 2740 feet
HIGH POINT:	10,150 feet
DIFFICULTY:	Moderate to challenging
TIME:	2.5 hours to 7.5 hours
FITNESS:	Hikers
FAMILY-FRIENDLY:	The hike is challenging, but you can choose a point of interest along the way for a shorter hike.
DOG-FRIENDLY:	No, dogs are prohibited.
AMENITIES:	Parking, restroom, maps
CONTACT/MAP:	US Forest Service
GPS:	40.57555°N, 111.68097°W
BEFORE YOU GO:	White Pine trailhead is popular; be prepared for crowds on weekends and evenings. Prime wildflower months are July and August. Popular location for backcountry skiing and snowshoeing. For winter travel, avalanche education and equipment are recommended.

GETTING THERE

Driving: From I-215, take exit 6 for 6200 S / UT 190 / Wasatch Boulevard and go southeast. Stay on Wasatch Boulevard for 4 miles, then go straight at the stoplight when it becomes UT 210 / Little Cottonwood Canyon Road. Follow UT 210 E up a winding canyon with stunning views for 5 miles to the White Pine trailhead and parking area on the right. Park along the highway if the lot is full. In 2022, the US Forest Service proposed a day-use fee, which will affect parking and use if implemented.

The 10.4-mile roundtrip hike to White Pine Lake is a lovely objective—the alpine lake view is a reward more than worthy of this distance and climb. It's also an ideal route for building fitness and stamina because the trail is brimming with points of interest like waterfalls, alpine meadows, and stunning vistas.

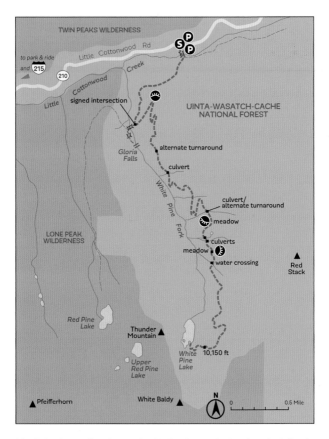

Until the last mile, the path climbs through the dappled shade of alternating quaking aspen and white fir forests. During the summer, dozens of wildflower species line the trail and color the mountainsides, and in autumn, the quaking aspen are ablaze with gold and strawberry-blond leaves.

The 5.2-mile trail that gradually ascends to White Pine Lake is a wide, easy-to-follow double track. Most of the route is rocky, with mud typically on some sections of trail. Be prepared for a lot of exposure in the last mile; bring appropriate clothing and plenty of water. The wildflowers and wet sections can mean a lot of bugs. Hiking with poles during any season are helpful.

GET MOVING

The trail starts behind the restrooms in the southwest corner of the parking lot. Look for a wood sign with the incorrect mileage to White Pine Lake (the sign indicates 4 miles, but the lake is more than 5 miles from the start). Descend onto the trail and keep left when the trail merges with an alternative trailhead access route.

At 0.1 mile, look for a trail map and a large wooden foot-bridge crossing Little Cottonwood Creek. Go right after crossing the bridge and start up the old access road. Ignore undeveloped side trails; throughout the hike, the wide foot-path is obvious and easy to follow.

The first mile is the most heavily trafficked. Despite rocky sections, it ascends gradually, gaining under 400 feet of elevation. Fields of flowers fill the understory—cow parsnip, net-tleleaf horsemint, and Richardson's geranium combine with flowering shrubs like Pacific ninebark and snowberry to create a visual feast.

Arrive at a major intersection with a sign and map at 1 mile. The path straight ahead goes toward Gloria Falls (see Go Farther) and Red Pine Lake. To continue to White Pine Lake, turn left up the rocky, wide lane, following the sign. At the first switch-back, the trail opens to a view of the Broads Fork Twin Peaks, Sunrise Peak, and Dromedary Peak.

Climb among paintbrush, cone flower, penstemon, flea-bane, and pearly everlasting. Around 2 miles, at 8500 feet elevation, the grade backs off and enters a mature white fir forest with lovely spots to rest or picnic. If you're tired, you could turn around here for a 4-mile roundtrip hike.

If you're continuing to White Pine Lake, you may encounter muddy sections and more bugs as the trail flattens. At

The aquamarine and tranquil waters of White Pine Lake

2.25 miles, cross a culvert. Enjoy the mellow wander until the route begins to gain elevation again at 2.75 miles. Cross another culvert at 2.9 miles and arrive at a pretty alpine meadow at 3.3 miles (9040 feet elevation). Your reward for all that climbing is an up-close view of Thunder Mountain and White Baldy. Take in the mountain views, and if you've had your fill of nature for the day, you could make this a turn-around spot for a 6.6-mile roundtrip adventure.

To visit White Pine Lake, keep following the trail south and encounter a pair of culverts. Arrive at another alpine meadow at 3.6 miles, this time with a view of Red Stack peak to the east. Soak in Red Stack's patchwork of periwinkle bluebells and golden arnica. From here, you could head back to the trailhead for a 7.4-mile roundtrip hike. Otherwise, keep following the trail to White Pine Lake.

Cross a drainage with running water (an inch or so deep) at around 4 miles. From the water crossing, you have a bit over a mile and about 850 feet of elevation gain to cover before reaching the lake. Climb a steep, shady trail lined with elephant's head and silky lupine flowers.

At 9700 feet elevation, the path moves out from the tree canopy and into a boulder field. Listen for Thunder Mountain's namesake starting at around 4.5 miles—you'll see the water raging over a steep talus face in the distance to the right.

Take the final ascent on a well-worn and sometimes rocky trail. Notice the change in foliage and look for rock-loving specimens like shrubby cinquefoil, Colorado blue columbine, and the electric-pink Parry's primrose.

Finally, the trail gains a ridge at the highest elevation point, 10,150 feet. From the ridge, descend 0.25 mile and arrive at White Pine Lake, 5.2 miles from the start.

The teal-blue, crystal-clear waters glimmer under White Baldy and Thunder Mountain. Find a picnic place, listen to the white-crowned sparrow's happy tune, and take some time to rejuvenate. When you're ready, retrace your steps back to the White Pine trailhead to complete your 10.4-mile alpine adventure.

GO FARTHER

Visit Gloria Falls, which flows from the White Pine Fork stream, for a 0.25-mile round-trip addition. The trail is steep and popular, with a big reward for a short climb.

To get there, start at the signed major intersection 1 mile into the main hike description and then continue straight for several hundred feet to cross a wood footbridge. Go several paces and cross two more small, wooden bridges. Begin a short, steep climb up the most well-worn trail and reach Gloria Falls at just over 0.1 mile from the signed intersection. Return on the same trail.

35 Cardiff Pass Trail

DISTANCE:	3.5 miles
ELEVATION GAIN:	1490 feet
HIGH POINT:	10,040 feet
DIFFICULTY:	Challenging
TIME:	3 hours
FITNESS:	Hikers
FAMILY-FRIENDLY:	The trail is very steep; only suitable for older children.
DOG-FRIENDLY:	No, dogs are prohibited.
AMENITIES:	Parking, restrooms, water
CONTACT/MAP:	Town of Alta
GPS:	40.58863°N, 111.64019°W
BEFORE YOU GO:	Weekends can be busy. Prime months for wildflowers are June through August. For winter travel, avalanche education and equipment are recommended.

GETTING THERE

Public Transit: Available only during ski season. Take UTA Ski Bus line 953 or 994 toward Snowbird/Alta and get off at the Goldminer's Daughter Lodge (Wildcat base area). **Driving:** From I-215, take exit 6 for 6200 S / UT 190 / Wasatch Boulevard and go southeast. Stay on Wasatch Boulevard for 4 miles, then go straight at the stoplight when it becomes UT 210 / Little Cottonwood Canyon Road. Follow UT 210 E up a

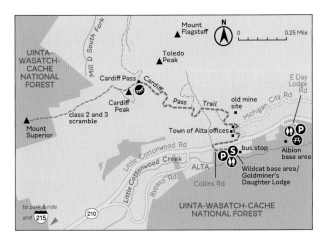

winding canyon with stunning views for 7.6 miles. Turn right on Collins Road and follow it to the Wildcat base area. During the ski season, expect parking fees for weekends and holidays.

When the snow melts in spring and early summer, Cardiff Pass Trail ascends a meadow blanketed with wildflowers. Snow patches often linger long in shady areas and at higher elevations. The steep hike up to the pass flies by with stunning views of Toledo Peak and Mount Superior. In winter, backcountry skiers use the trail as an access point to reach the surrounding peaks. The ridge gained at Cardiff Pass is the Big Cottonwood/Little Cottonwood Divide; continuing west on this ridge will take you along the standard hiking route for the summit of Mount Superior (see Go Farther).

GET MOVING

Start at the Wildcat base area (elevation 8530 feet) and walk north on Collins Road for 0.2 mile. Turn right on UT 210 / Little Cottonwood Canyon Road and go 0.2 mile to Michigan City Road. Head left up steep Michigan City Road and pass the Town of Alta Municipal Offices and Alta Justice Court on

the left. When the road forks, go right for a couple of hundred feet and then turn left off Michigan City Road onto a wide dirt track. Climb the double-track trail through sparse aspens and pines for 0.1 mile. When a steep path appears on your left, keep right and keep climbing.

As the trail trends left, look for an old mine site to the right. Reach a junction at 1.2 miles. The trail on the right leads to Toledo Peak; you should continue straight on the Cardiff Pass Trail, trending uphill and west.

Keep climbing and ignore another steep trail to the left at 1.4 miles. Arrive at a welcome, flat meadow below Toledo Peak. In the late spring and early summer, paintbrush, aster, and alpine sage paint the landscape green, crimson, gold, and lavender. From the meadow, you have a clear view of the final 400-vertical-foot scramble up to Cardiff Pass.

Gain the 10,000-plus-foot ridge at 1.75 miles from the trailhead. A scenic view of Snowbird and Alta ski resorts dominates the southern skyline, while Mill D South and Big Cottonwood Canyon fill out the north. Soak in the aerial panoramic of dramatic peaks and jagged crags before returning the way you came.

GO FARTHER

From Cardiff Pass, you can follow a steep, rocky trail along the east ridge of Mount Superior for 1.1 miles to the summit. It's a challenging traverse that mostly stays to the north side of the crest, with some steep sections requiring Class 2 to 3 scrambles. It's easy to get turned around or disoriented here; consult a hike description that includes a detailed play-by-play for navigating the east ridge. Some people may feel more comfortable hiring a guide for the Class 3 scrambles.

Opposite: *Arrowleaf balsamroot and buckwheat blanket the slopes near Cardiff Pass in late spring.*

36 Albion Basin to Cecret Lake

DISTANCE:	5 miles
ELEVATION GAIN:	1230 feet
HIGH POINT:	9880 feet
DIFFICULTY:	Moderate to challenging
TIME:	3.5 hours
FITNESS:	Hikers, runners
FAMILY-FRIENDLY:	Yes, wildlife and flora galore. Option for a shorter hike with alternate paid parking.
DOG-FRIENDLY:	No, dogs are prohibited.
AMENITIES:	Parking, restrooms, water, maps, interpretive signs, campground, picnic tables, provisions at Alta Camp Store (limited days, noon to 6:00 PM)
CONTACT/MAP:	US Forest Service; Town of Alta
GPS:	40.59108°N, 111.62830°W
BEFORE YOU GO:	Albion Basin is legendary for its annual wildflower showcase; June through August are the prime months. Parking at Albion base area (and Wildcat base area) is free. Parking at Catherine Pass trailhead or Cecret Lake trailhead costs $10 per vehicle. During winter, the hiking area is part of Alta Ski Area's terrain. Little Cottonwood Canyon is Salt Lake's watershed—absolutely no swimming in Cecret Lake.

GETTING THERE

Driving: From I-215, take exit 6 for 6200 S / UT 190 / Wasatch Boulevard and go southeast. Stay on Wasatch Boulevard for 4 miles, then go straight at the stoplight when it becomes UT 210 / Little Cottonwood Canyon Road. Follow UT 210 E up a winding canyon with stunning views for 8.2 miles. Turn right on E. Day Lodge Road and drive 0.2 mile until it ends at the Albion base area parking lot.

Albion Basin displays a treasure trove of biological diversity and pristine mountain beauty. Even though it spans just three

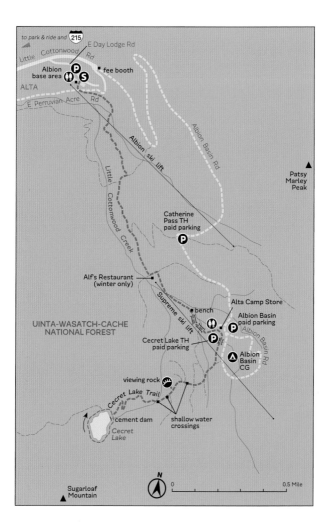

acres, it's home to more than 80 species of birds, plus mammals like moose, mule deer, bobcats, foxes, badgers, marmots, and Uinta ground squirrels. And with more than 400 plant species—at least 120 of them wildflowers—it's also the

Wildflowers in every color of the rainbow bloom in Albion Basin from June through August.

perfect location for the annual wildflower festival hosted by the Cottonwood Canyons Foundation.

As the central connection point for Little Cottonwood Canyon, Big Cottonwood Canyon, and American Fork Canyon, Albion Basin's geography is dramatic. It's an area hub for year-round recreational pursuits, including alpine skiing, backcountry skiing, snowshoeing, hiking, and rock climbing. Since it contains the headwaters of Little Cottonwood Creek, it's also one of the wettest places in Utah, providing Salt Lake City with about 15 percent of its drinking water.

The elevation is approximately 4000 feet higher than most of Salt Lake, so it's significantly cooler, making it an excellent option for hot days. Bring clothing appropriate for colder temps and potential thunderstorms.

GET MOVING

Start at the Albion base area parking lot. Locate the information kiosk to the left of the public restrooms and walk past it on a gravel road. Go left, following the sign for Albion Basin and Cecret Lake. Cross E Perruvian Acre Road and start ascending on a gentle-grade double track through a meadow of grasses, white sage, and willows.

Eventually, the way narrows, and at 0.25 mile, it moves under the Albion ski lift. Follow the switchbacks as they zig in and out of a forest of white firs. Encounter a T intersection at 0.5 mile and go right. Then, after a few hundred feet, go left at a fork.

The next half mile is a wildflower mecca. Nature is the most skilled of all artists, playing with complementary hues and heights for a scene so sensational it steals your breath. Play the flower identification game and search for a kaleidoscope of colors: splitleaf paintbrush in red, hot-pink wild sticky geranium, fuchsia fireweed, Wyoming paintbrush in orange, golden arrowleaf balsamroot, green cone flower, fringed bluebells, lavender nettleleaf horsemint, lupine and fleabane in shades of purple, and bright-white Jacob's ladder.

Halfway through the wildflower haven, come to a signed fork and veer right. (Left is the half-mile approach to Catherine Pass trailhead, with paid parking and an alternative start.) Encounter a T intersection at 1 mile, just before Alf's Restaurant (closed during the summer). Go left to ascend a short, steep gravel road for several paces, and then turn right to skirt around the restaurant. The Supreme ski lift is visible down to the right. Past the restaurant, the gravel road reverts to a dirt hiking trail.

Amble along the well-shaded trail under a canopy of white firs. At 1.3 miles, come to a streamside cove with a perfect resting bench. Walk along a boardwalk leading to a signed intersection and then go left to cross two more small boardwalks.

At 1.5 miles, after gaining more than 700 feet of elevation, reach the Cecret Lake trailhead and Albion Basin campground parking lot (alternate start with paid entrance). Go left at the parking lot and walk on the road until you reach pit toilets on the left. Turn right onto a dirt trail that passes a picnic area, and then pass the Alta Camp Store just before a four-way junction.

Go right at the four-way junction onto Cecret Lake Trail and cross a small wood footbridge. Follow the well-shaded trail to a T intersection with a wide, multiuse dirt road and go right. Ignore the numerous small tracks intersecting the path; the dirt road is evident and easy to follow.

At 2 miles, cross some shallow water and veer left to avoid entering a couple of private driveways. Then look for a small side trail on the right leading to a viewing rock. Ramble to the vista for a 360-degree panorama of Wasatch crags and peaks—Cardiff Peak and Flagstaff Mountain to the northwest; Patsy Marley Peak, Mount Wolverine, and Mount Tuscarora to the northeast; and Devils Castle and Sugarloaf Mountain to the south.

Return to the main trail, cross another two patches of shallow water, and begin the final ascent. The trail becomes a steep, rocky single track, gaining 300 feet of elevation in 0.3 mile.

Arrive at Cecret Lake at 2.5 miles (elevation 9880 feet). Find a pleasant place to listen to birds and watch for wildlife, or walk the quick lakeside loop (see Go Farther). When you're ready, retrace the route back to the trailhead to complete your 5-mile journey.

GO FARTHER

Take the 0.4-mile loop around Cecret Lake for an opportunity to traverse its less busy eastern and southern shores. Use caution: there are several exposed sections with a steep drop into the lake.

Begin by going left at the lake to cross a cement dam. At 0.1 mile, scramble over a narrow cliffside passage with the water a dozen feet below. When you reach a talus field blanketed in wildflowers, keep to the well-defined path as it traverses boulders. Continue to trend right to stay near the lake and complete the loop.

Next page: *The moon rises above the foothills of Draper (Hike 38).*

DRAPER

From Lone Peak, which towers majestically over the city of Draper, five tributaries flow to the Jordan River. Before the arrival of pioneers, these five waterways nourished pristine marshlands and bogs teeming with willows. Native peoples called the area *Sivogah*, which means "willows."

When the first homesteaders arrived in the mid-1800s, they drained the marshes and bogs to create farmland, constructing extensive canals, dams, and irrigation systems. Today, stables and pastures scattered among all the modern houses are a reminder of the area's homesteading past.

Although irrigation has dramatically altered the landscape, the Draper foothills remain a thriving habitat for native creatures. There's plenty for nature lovers to enjoy in Draper. Walk the Bear Canyon Suspension Bridge (Hike 39), and look for sage hens, wild turkeys, and grouse, as well as large mammals like deer, elk, mountain goats, mountain sheep, coyotes, and (rarely) mountain lions.

Or visit the ponds and riparian habitat in Mehraban Wetlands Park (Hike 37) for a glimpse of what Draper's geography may have looked like in centuries past. This little slice of wilderness is a hidden gem surrounded by development. Even though the invasive Russian olive trees now outnumber the native willows, the area still provides a critical home for countless bird species.

37 Mehraban Wetlands Park

DISTANCE:	1.1-mile loop
ELEVATION GAIN:	90 feet
HIGH POINT:	4500 feet
DIFFICULTY:	Easy
TIME:	30 minutes
FITNESS:	Walkers, runners
FAMILY-FRIENDLY:	Yes, the paved portion is stroller-friendly and ADA-accessible.
DOG-FRIENDLY:	Yes, on-leash. Poop bags and waste bins at the trailhead.
AMENITIES:	Parking, bike rack, interpretive signs, fishing, birding
CONTACT/MAP:	Draper Parks and Recreation
GPS:	40.53642°N, 111.86655°W
BEFORE YOU GO:	Park hours are from dawn to 10:00 PM. A fishing license is required for people over twelve years old.

GETTING THERE

Public Transit: Take TRAX Blue Line to Kimballs Lane Station. Request a UTA On Demand ride from the TRAX station to the Mehraban Wetlands Park entrance. Or, to walk the 0.3 mile to the wetlands, go north on 700 E for 0.1 mile and then turn right on Meadow Wood Drive. Travel for 0.2 mile and turn right on S. Willow Wood Drive. Look for the entrance, a paved pedestrian way on the right. **Bike Route:** Use the Salt Lake City & County Bikeways Map to plot a route to the trailhead. **Driving:** From I-15, take exit 292 for UT 175 E, and go east on 11400 S for 1.2 miles. Turn right on 700 E and drive for 0.4 mile, followed by a left on Meadow Wood Drive. After 0.2 mile, go right on S. Willow Wood Drive and then take the next right on 880 E. The wetland parking area is on the right.

You'll want to bring your binoculars and identification guide for this one. The Mehraban Wetlands Park, with its dappled shade and mellow paths, is pleasant to visit year-round—but birders are especially rewarded in late spring through summer. The preserved riparian habitat is a bird sanctuary for numerous species, including flycatchers, orioles, grosbeaks, chickadees, and American robins.

The wetlands harbor an unexpected array of biodiversity amid heavy urban development. Two ponds feature fishing docks and countless pleasant picnic locations. A shelter from encroaching industry, Mehraban Wetlands Park's thriving vegetation, abundant animal life, and freedom from noise pollution make it an enchanting place to soak up some nature.

The route described here starts at the parking lot trailhead, follows the paved pedestrian path until it ends at the first pond, loops around both ponds, and then picks up the paved trail to the opposite end of the park.

GET MOVING

From the parking lot, locate the paved pedestrian avenue to the south. Begin a gentle descent alongside grasses and shrubs—keep an eye out for showy milkweed, an essential

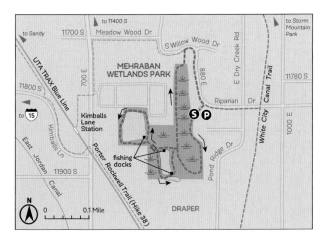

Peaceful fishing docks surround ponds in Mehraban Wetlands Park.

food source for the monarch butterfly. At 0.1 mile, the lane curves under a canopy of mature Fremont cottonwoods.

When the path forks at 0.25 mile, go left toward the lower pond, where mallards and Canada geese love to gather. Encounter a pristine viewing and fishing dock on the left and continue toward the second pond.

The paved trail ends at 0.3 mile, just after crossing a wood footbridge. When the path forks in front of another fishing dock, go right to circle the upper pond on a single-track dirt trail. The reeds and pond grasses thicken as the track veers left.

When the trail moves along the upper pond's west edge, gaze east at the highest visible spire, Lone Peak. Finish the loop and cross the wood footbridge for a second time. After the bridge, go right onto a narrow dirt path to walk the shady loop around the lower pond. Another fishing and observation dock halfway around the pond is a fun place to stop, and you can find ample picnic spots underneath the pleasant, shady trees.

Finish the lower pond loop at 0.75 mile, and go right on the paved path for several paces. When the lane forks, go left to begin a gentle 0.25-mile climb until the trail ends on S. Willow Wood Drive (elevation 4500 feet, public transit entrance).

To return to the trailhead, turn right on S. Willow Wood Drive and then take an immediate right onto 880 E. After 0.1 mile, look for the trailhead and parking on the right. (Alternatively, you can retrace the paved pathway through the wetlands for half a mile back to the trailhead.)

GO FARTHER

If you want to tack on a few extra miles, the 4-mile White City Canal Trail is a great option. A short 0.5 mile walk north to Storm Mountain Park provides a panorama of Mount Olympus (Hike 20), Broads Fork Twin Peaks, Bells Canyon (Hike 28), and Lone Peak. Walking another 2.1 miles north on the White City Trail will bring you to a massive and enclosed pedestrian bridge spanning Dimple Dell Regional Park (Hike 26).

To reach the White City Trail from the Mehraban Wetlands trailhead, walk east on Riparian Drive for 0.1 mile and turn left on the paved trail. From here, the canal trail runs for 3.3 miles to the north and 0.7 mile to the south.

38 Porter Rockwell Trail and Draper Canal

DISTANCE:	7.2-mile loop
ELEVATION GAIN:	220 feet
HIGH POINT:	4650 feet
DIFFICULTY:	Easy
TIME:	3.5 hours
FITNESS:	Walkers, runners

FAMILY-FRIENDLY:	Yes, paved paths are ADA-accessible and suitable for strollers.
DOG-FRIENDLY:	Yes, on-leash. Poop bags and waste bins throughout.
AMENITIES:	Parking, restrooms, drinking water, playgrounds, picnic areas, pavilions, sports courts
CONTACT/MAP:	Draper Parks and Recreation
GPS:	40.52423°N, 111.85393°W
BEFORE YOU GO:	Draper City Park hours are 6:00 AM to 10:00 PM. Porter Rockwell Trail closes at 10:00 PM. Wheadon Farm Park hours are 9:00 AM to 10:00 PM.

GETTING THERE

Public Transit: Take TRAX Blue Line to Draper Town Center Station. Go south to cross Pioneer Road and walk toward the Draper Library. Then turn right into Draper City Park and go east on the park's northern perimeter to reach the northeast parking lot. **Bike Route:** Use the Salt Lake City & County Bikeways Map to plot a route to the trailhead. **Driving:** From I-15, take exit 291 for UT 71 / 12300 S and travel west for 1.4 miles. Turn right on 900 E, followed by a left on Pioneer Road, and continue 0.7 mile. At the roundabout, take the first exit onto 1300 E and then an immediate right on Constitution Avenue. Look for Draper City Park's northeast parking lot on the left.

The Porter Rockwell Trail gets its name from an infamous Mormon pioneer known for his gunfighting skills and long hair. Orrin Porter Rockwell served as a bodyguard for The Church of Jesus Christ of Latter-day Saints church leaders, including Brigham Young, in the mid-1800s. He was appointed as deputy marshal of Salt Lake City in 1849. A feared mercenary in his era, he was also known as a destroying angel of the Mormon Church. In a public address in 1869 he admitted, "I never killed anyone who didn't need killing."

The walk described here highlights a scenic and quiet 3.5-mile stretch of the Porter Rockwell Trail between Draper City Park and Wheadon Farm Park—but the paved, multi-use path stretches from Sandy to Lehi for nearly 19 miles.

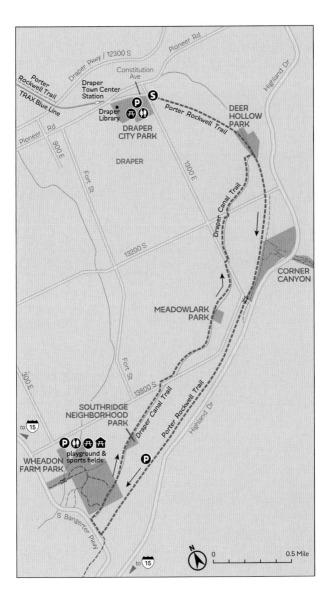

Winter walkers stroll the Draper Canal Trail. (Photo by Denise Heil)

On this hike, you'll follow a sizeable, clockwise loop, moving south on Porter Rockwell Trail and then returning along the Draper Canal Trail. Folks looking for a shorter stroll can choose to park at either Draper City Park or Wheadon Farm Park (see Go Farther) and just follow the route for a mile or two. The Draper Canal Trail is ideal for strollers and wheelchairs, with a more consistent and gradual grade than the Porter Rockwell Trail.

GET MOVING

Begin at the northeast parking lot of Draper City Park (elevation 4530 feet). Use the crosswalk to cross 1300 E, and look for the large, wooden Porter Rockwell Trail sign. Over the next 3.5 miles, the paved trail moves through shady canopies of mature maple and elm trees and fields of big sage, white sage, rabbitbrush, and wildflowers.

Pass Deer Hollow Park on the left at 0.75 mile, and then look for the Draper Canal Trail (return route) on the right. For now, go straight to stay on the Porter Rockwell Trail. Cross 13200 S at 1.1 miles. (A sign for the Bunny Bradley Trail soon appears; it leads to Corner Canyon, a popular mountain biking destination.)

Stay on the paved Porter Rockwell Trail, ignoring several neighborhood access trails. Pass the base of Corner Canyon and its trail networks on the left at about 1.5 miles. At 1.75 miles, cross 1300 E again, then traverse next to peaceful homes and lovely gardens as the path moves through a series of gentle, rolling hills. At 2.9 miles, reach the highest elevation point (4650 feet), just before passing a small neighborhood parking lot to the right at 3 miles.

The trail exits onto 300 E / S. Bangerter Parkway at 3.5 miles. From here, go right toward Wheadon Farm Park and the Draper Canal Trail, following the trail signs. (The Porter Rockwell Trail continues on the other side of S. Bangerter Parkway beyond the overpass; see Go Farther.)

Head downhill on a sidewalk for several hundred feet and turn right onto the signed, paved Draper Canal Trail at 3.7 miles. Walk several paces and encounter a track on the left that leads to Wheadon Farm Park (see Go Farther). For now, keep ambling on the Draper Canal Trail.

As you head northeast, Wasatch spires create a sensational backdrop, including the Broads Fork Twin Peaks and Mount Olympus (Hike 20). This section of the Draper Canal

Trail also features spacious properties, some with farm animals, a reminder of the area's homesteading past. The horses are a highlight.

At 4.3 miles, pass Southridge Park on the right. After crossing 13800 S at 4.7 miles, look for Meadowlark Park on the right about a half a mile later. Cross 1300 E at 5.6 miles, and at 6.4 miles, connect with the Porter Rockwell Trail.

Turn left on Porter Rockwell Trail and retrace your steps for 0.7 mile to the trailhead, which marks the completion of your 7.2-mile loop.

GO FARTHER

Meander the 1.5 miles of walking paths in Wheadon Farm Park, which was a working family farm for decades. In 1997, Gene Wheadon donated the land to Utah Open Lands, a nonprofit conservation easement association. When Salt Lake County purchased the land from Utah Open Lands in 2008, the county agreed to keep the land open to the public, honor its agricultural heritage, and comply with conservation easement requirements.

Today, the 64-acre plot of land is a tribute to Gene Wheadon, an excellent steward who loved the land and wanted it preserved for ages to come. Wheadon Farm Park features open space for wildlife habitat, urban farming, a farm-themed playground, pavilions, sports fields, and interpretive signs. It's a great place to bring children, and adults will enjoy themselves too.

And if you want to add even more miles, you can continue north or south along the 19-mile-long Porter Rockwell Trail. The 10.5 miles south of Wheadon Farm Park often run parallel to I-15. The 5 miles north of Draper City Park parallel the TRAX, but this section does not connect to the trailhead at Draper City Park, instead requiring a mile or so of urban routefinding.

39 Bear Canyon Suspension Bridge

DISTANCE:	4.4-mile loop
ELEVATION GAIN:	670 feet
HIGH POINT:	5250 feet
DIFFICULTY:	Moderate
TIME:	2 hours
FITNESS:	Hikers, runners
FAMILY-FRIENDLY:	Yes
DOG-FRIENDLY:	Yes, on-leash. Poop bags and waste bins at Orson Smith trailhead. The route accesses trails within the watershed, where dogs are prohibited: respect signs and dog-area boundaries.
AMENITIES:	Parking, restrooms, water, picnic benches, trail information
CONTACT/MAP:	Draper Parks and Recreation
GPS:	40.52204˚N, 111.83389˚W
BEFORE YOU GO:	Orson Smith trailhead hours are 6:00 AM to 10:00 PM. Popular in the evenings and on weekends. Rare rattlesnake and mountain lion encounters. For winter travel, avalanche education and equipment are recommended.

GETTING THERE

Public Transit: Take TRAX Blue Line to Draper Town Center Station. Request a UTA On Demand ride from the TRAX station to Orson Smith trailhead. **Bike Route:** Use the Salt Lake City & County Bikeways Map to plot a route to the trailhead. **Driving:** From I-15, take exit 291 for UT 71 / 12300 S and travel east for 1.3 miles. Turn right on 900 E and then take an immediate left on Pioneer Road. Reach a traffic circle in 0.6 mile, take the second exit to stay on Pioneer Road, and drive for 1 mile. Turn right on 2000 E / Highland Drive; the trailhead is on the left in 0.3 mile.

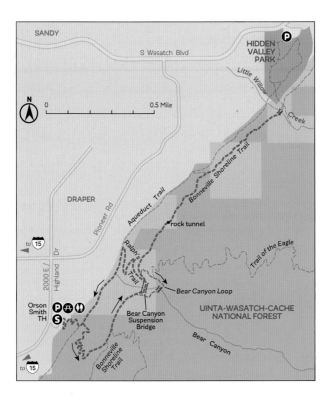

This route explores two of the five tributaries that flow from Lone Peak to the Jordan River: Little Willow Creek and a spring-fed stream in Bear Canyon. A hike highlight is the Bear Canyon Suspension Bridge, which spans 185 feet across Bear Canyon. The marvelous wood and metal structure is perched high above the canyon floor, and the view west is a rugged vision of the Oquirrh Mountains.

The trail begins at the Orson Smith trailhead and connects the suspension bridge to Little Willow Creek on the Bonneville Shoreline Trail (BST). The first mile or so offers little to no shade, which is not ideal for hot days. During

Hiker and canine enjoy the view from Bear Canyon Suspension Bridge.

snow or ice conditions, micro-traction spikes and poles are recommended. Ample trail signs make this area easy to navigate.

GET MOVING

Locate a set of wood steps near the restrooms and trail information bulletin to begin your hike. Ascend the well-worn dirt switchbacks up a consistent grade, climbing through fields of Gambel oak, big sage, and rabbitbrush punctuated by granite boulders.

After gaining nearly 200 feet of elevation in 0.25 mile, the path intercepts the Aqueduct Trail at a T intersection. Go left, followed by an almost immediate right at the "bridge loop" sign. Continue up well-worn switchbacks to gain a stunner view of Blackridge (Hike 42) and the Oquirrh Mountains to the west. At 0.7 mile, when the trail forks, turn left on the Bonneville Shoreline Trail.

Veer left through a series of forks, remaining on the BST. Take in the expansive views to the north of Salt Lake City, Ensign Peak (Hike 7), City Creek Canyon (Hike 8), Red Butte (Hike 9), Neffs Canyon (Hike 19), Mount Olympus (Hike 20), and Heughs Canyon (Hike 21).

The footpath levels out and widens, and just before the suspension bridge, the trail forks. Go left to remain on the BST (right is the Go Farther route). Cross the bridge and marvel at its architecture while floating above Bear Canyon.

A few hundred feet past the bridge, go right to avoid descending on Ralph's Trail. When the track diverges again at 1.1 miles, go straight toward Little Willow Creek (right is the Go Farther route). The next mile is a pleasant, mostly flat stroll on the BST.

At 1.4 miles, the walkway narrows and moves beneath an aesthetic rock tunnel. After the rock tunnel, mature bigtooth maples, Gambel oaks, and alderleaf mountain mahogany provide the first substantial shade of the journey.

A small byway merges with the BST at 1.7 miles; continue going straight. Just before Little Willow Creek, at 2.1 miles, gain the hike's high point (elevation 5250 feet). At 2.2 miles, after a short descent, cross Little Willow Creek on a wood footbridge. Climb wooden steps to a wide, gravel path—left goes toward Hidden Valley Park; straight ahead, the BST enters a no-dog zone. Turn around here and retrace your steps back toward the suspension bridge.

Reach the Bear Canyon Loop (see Go Farther) at 3.3 miles. To return to the trailhead, go straight for 0.1 mile and then turn right to descend on Ralph's Trail, following the signs. Lose 190 feet of elevation over the next 0.3 mile as the trail switchbacks down. At 3.7 miles from the start, where Ralph's Trail intersects the Aqueduct Trail, turn left.

Stay on the wide, flat Aqueduct Trail for 0.4 mile and then turn right at 4.1 miles to return to the trailhead and complete your 4.4-mile journey.

GO FARTHER

The Bear Canyon Loop adds 0.4 mile as it climbs a ridge and then dips down into the lush woods of Bear Canyon. Dogs are not permitted on this trail, so plan accordingly.

After returning from Little Willow Creek, keep an eye out for the Bear Canyon Loop sign. Turn left at the sign to start the loop. Climb a rocky and steep passage, gaining 140 feet of elevation in just over 0.1 mile. Reach a fork at the highest elevation point (5340 feet) and go straight to pass a granite boulder outcrop.

The trail descends into a shady canopy of mature trees. At 0.2 mile, cross a footbridge and climb out of the forest. Intersect the BST at 0.3 mile, go right, and cross the Bear Canyon Suspension Bridge. At 0.4 mile, go left on Ralph's Trail at the signed junction to return to the trailhead.

Next page: A pedestrian underpass on the Oquirrh Lake Loop (Hike 41)

WEST JORDAN TO HERRIMAN

West Jordan was settled by pioneers in the mid-1800s, and the city maintains a distinctly family-oriented flavor. Meander past quaint West Jordan neighborhoods and backyard gardens on the quiet Bingham Creek Trail (Hike 40).

For a more urban jaunt, head to the master-planned community of Daybreak to explore the miles of paths surrounding Oquirrh Lake (Hike 41). The last stop on the TRAX Red Line, Daybreak, demonstrates what well-managed population growth in the Salt Lake City suburbs can look like. It offers a variety of housing, from mixed-use apartments and townhouses to large lakefront family homes. An expansive network of paved corridors for non-motorized transportation connects the community.

Herriman is Salt Lake County's most southwestern city, located in the foothills of the Oquirrh Mountains. Climb Blackridge (Hike 42) and you'll be gifted with a spectacular panorama of the Wasatch Range, granting you a fresh perspective on many of the hikes featured in this guide.

All three trails in this section are easy to access using the TRAX Red Line. The Oquirrh Lake Loop and Blackridge hikes are within UTA's On Demand zone, which makes getting from the TRAX station to the trailhead a snap. Additionally, each trail is either fully stroller- and ADA-accessible or has paved walking options.

40 Bingham Creek Trail

DISTANCE:	3.2 miles
ELEVATION GAIN:	190 feet
HIGH POINT:	4790 feet
DIFFICULTY:	Easy
TIME:	2 hours
FITNESS:	Walkers, runners
FAMILY-FRIENDLY:	Yes, the entire paved trail is excellent for strollers and is ADA-accessible.
DOG-FRIENDLY:	Yes, on-leash. Poop bags and waste bins throughout.
AMENITIES:	Parking, restrooms (open May to September), playgrounds, pavilions, and picnic tables (at adjacent parks)
CONTACT/MAP:	West Jordan Parks Department
GPS:	40.57719°N, 111.99895°W
BEFORE YOU GO:	There is very little shade, which makes this trail an excellent cool-weather hike. The trail moves through neighborhoods—respect people's homes and gardens. Popular with cyclists.

GETTING THERE

Public Transit: Take TRAX Red Line to 4800 West / Old Bingham Highway Station. Turn left on 4800 W and go south 0.3 mile. Turn left on Skye Drive and look for the trailhead on the left in 0.2 mile. **Bike Route:** Use the Salt Lake City & County Bikeways Map to plot a route to the trailhead. **Driving:** From I-15, take exit 295 for UT 209 / 9000 S and go west for 4.8 miles. Turn left on Old Bingham Highway and drive for 0.8 mile. After the TRAX station, turn left on 4800 W and continue for 0.3 mile. Turn left on Skye Drive, and after 0.2 mile, look for the trailhead on the left.

A deer crossing the trail on its way to Bingham Creek is physical proof that small ribbons of wilderness within suburbia are sources of life for our fellow creatures. The deer that wander here are a testament to the importance of leaving areas unadulterated by human development.

With its proximity to the TRAX station and smooth, white-washed pavement, Bingham Creek Trail is an approachable outdoor access point for users from all walks of life. Sandwiched between serene neighborhoods and a golf course, the path runs parallel to a thick band of biodiversity surrounding seasonally flowing Bingham Creek. The trail is tranquil and surprisingly free from noise pollution.

The route as described here starts at the trailhead across from the Glenmoor Field baseball diamond. You'll follow the path west before looping back to the trailhead and then following the lane east until it ends at Vista West Park.

GET MOVING

Locate the paved pedestrian path at the west end of the parking lot. Cross Skye Drive and head right (west) on Bingham Creek Trail. The barren mountainside of Kennecott Copper

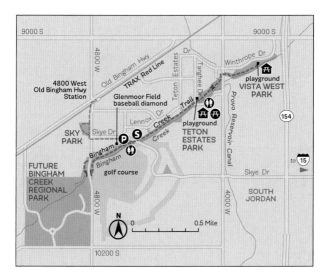

Drought-tolerant home gardens along the Bingham Creek Trail

Mine is in the foreground as you walk, and White Pine Peak, West Mountain, and Clipper Peak form the Oquirrh Mountains backdrop.

This section gains about 50 feet of elevation in 0.5 mile and takes you to an underpass. Go through the tunnel and encounter a fork in the trail. Left goes toward the future Bingham Creek Regional Park, formerly known as the Welby Pit. The Salt Lake County master plan for the park includes fields, walking paths, pavilions, a disc golf course, restrooms, and parking. The area is closed until construction is complete, so go right and walk a few hundred feet to reach 4800 W and the hike's high point (elevation 4790 feet). Then turn around and retrace your steps on the Bingham Creek Trail.

Cross Skye Drive again, and at 1 mile from the start, encounter the trailhead for a second time. Stay on Bingham Creek Trail and keep walking east. Relish the sweeping panorama of Wasatch Mountains: Grandeur Peak (Hike 15), Mount Aire (Hike 16), Mount Olympus (Hike 20), Lone Peak, and farthest south, glimpses of Mount Timpanogos.

The water flow at seasonal Bingham Creek varies, but the drainage hosts Gambel oaks, velvet ash, and occasional catalpa trees even when dry. Familiar mountain shrubs such as big sage, fourwing saltbush, fragrant sumac, and rubber rabbitbrush grow along the walkway.

It's easy to stay on course; keep to the paved path. At 1.1 miles, notice cement stairs used for neighborhood access on your left. After the stairs, charming backyard gardens line the walkway. Garden motifs range from desert-inspired flowering ornamentals to small orchards and vegetable gardens

Saunter past another set of stairs at 1.4 miles and then cross Targhee Drive to enter Teton Estates Park. The pedestrian walkway becomes a sidewalk as it traverses Teton Estates Park and then crosses Provo Reservoir Canal on a cement bridge at 1.7 miles. Shortly after the canal, the sidewalk forks; go right.

Use the crosswalk to cross 4000 W, and keep heading east on the paved pedestrian passage. Mature Fremont cottonwood groves change the character of the trail over the next 0.3 mile. At 2.1 miles from the start, the pavement ends at Vista West Park.

Find a quiet place to picnic under the pavilion or a shade tree. When you're ready, return to the trailhead on Bingham Creek Trail to complete your 3.2-mile journey.

GO FURTHER

Reduce greenhouse gas emissions and embark on a true urban adventure by using public transportation to reach the trailhead.

Riding TRAX to Bingham Creek Trail is delightful. The walk from the TRAX station to the trailhead moves through tranquil neighborhoods on the sidewalks of quiet roads. Plan for a pitstop at Skye Park on 4800 W on the way to or from the trailhead. It sports restrooms, a big grassy field, and a large playground.

41 Oquirrh Lake Loop

DISTANCE:	3.2-mile loop
ELEVATION GAIN:	80 feet
HIGH POINT:	4810 feet
DIFFICULTY:	Easy
TIME:	2 hours
FITNESS:	Walkers, runners
FAMILY-FRIENDLY:	Yes, the flat, paved trail is stroller- and ADA-accessible.
DOG-FRIENDLY:	Yes, on-leash. Poop bags and waste bins throughout.
AMENITIES:	Parking, restrooms, fishing, birding, benches, playground, grocery store, restaurants
CONTACT/MAP:	Daybreak Parks and Recreation
GPS:	40.54621°N, 112.00318°W
BEFORE YOU GO:	Open dawn to dusk. Swimming in the lake is prohibited. The use of watercraft is for Daybreak residents only (with a permit). Not much shade.

GETTING THERE

Public Transit: Take TRAX Red Line to Daybreak Parkway Station. Request a UTA On Demand ride from the TRAX station to The Beach Club / Daybreak Boat Dock. **Bike Route:** Use the Salt Lake City & County Bikeways Map to plot a route to the trailhead. **Driving:** From I-15, take exit 292 for UT 175 / 11400 S and go west on 11400 S for 4.6 miles until it becomes W. Daybreak Parkway. Go another 0.6 mile, and at the roundabout, take the third exit onto Kestrel Ridge Road. After 0.2 mile, turn right onto S. Kestrel Rise Road, followed by a right onto Daybreak Rim Way. The parking area is on the left and has electric-vehicle charging stations. To access the trail, walk northwest on S. Kestrel Rise Road to reach The Beach Club / Daybreak Boat Dock. There is also street parking along the lake.

The master-planned community of Daybreak has an extensive trail network, which the public is welcome to enjoy. Circle the unique, manufactured shape of Oquirrh Lake on the paved Oquirrh Lake Loop Trail. This delightful, easy path meanders past colorful homes, charming landscaping, and sweeping Wasatch Range vistas. The lake is ideal for birding—it's easy to spot the mallards, Canada geese, and other resident species like the yellow-headed blackbird, American coot, killdeer, and American kestrel.

The route as described here starts at the Daybreak Boat Dock; however, any starting point along the loop is as good as another. Parks, restrooms, and dozens of benches are scattered along the path, and SoDa Row's restaurants and access to grocery stores make it easy to pick up picnic items along the way. In early summer, there can be a lot of lakeside bugs, but the pavement and exposure make this a perfect cold-weather hike.

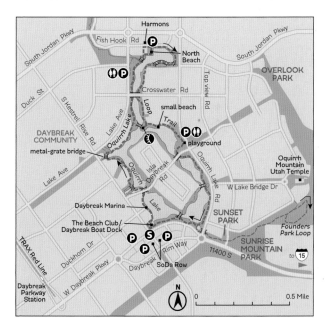

Kayakers on Oquirrh Lake

GET MOVING

From the viewing balcony of The Beach Club/Daybreak Boat Dock, look for the paved pedestrian trail to the right and follow it toward the water. After several hundred feet, it merges with another paved path; veer left to begin the 3.2-mile clockwise loop. Countless side trails, sidewalks, and neighborhood access pathways intercept the Oquirrh Lake Loop Trail. When in doubt, take the paved loop that veers toward the lake.

Pass the Daybreak Marina and move through an underpass. After several hundred feet, go right to cross the lake on a large wood-and-metal pedestrian bridge. At 0.5 mile, cross a tiered water structure on a metal-grate bridge, and then go right to stay on Oquirrh Lake Loop Trail.

When the track forks at 0.9 mile, veer left. (To reduce the loop length by 1.2 miles, go right to cross a pedestrian bridge and then turn right onto the Oquirrh Loop Lake Trail.) At 1 mile, the footpath goes through an underpass. At the next fork, go right and at 1.2 miles, pass restrooms and parking on Lake Avenue. Cross a small footbridge at 1.25 miles and continue for several hundred feet to Fish Hook Road. Harmons grocery store, a good spot for refreshments, is visible straight ahead.

Go right as the way runs parallel to Fish Hook Road and passes North Beach. Stay right, continuing to follow the lake. This section has several stands of young black poplar, velvet ash, and river birch trees; in time, they will grow to provide a canopy of shade. Cross another small footbridge at 1.5 miles.

After the footbridge, the passage forks; go right to walk a short section of boardwalk nestled among cattails.

At 1.9 miles, the pathway leads back to a familiar underpass, this time on the opposite side of the lake. Reach the hike's high point (elevation 4810 feet) at 2.1 miles, with a spectacular view of the Oquirrh Mountains to the west, Mount Timpanogos to the southeast, and Lone Peak to the east. After the viewpoint, stay left to avoid crossing a footbridge and then pass by a small beach.

Restrooms, followed by a playground, can be found on the left at 2.3 miles. At 2.5 miles, cut under Isla Daybreak Road via an underpass and then follow the path a short distance to walk under a picturesque pedestrian bridge. A section of gravel at 3 miles leads to a fork; go right, followed by another immediate right (left goes toward Sunrise Mountain Park, see Go Farther).

At the next pedestrian bridge underpass, turn around and look east for a Wasatch Mountain vista. To finish the 3.2-mile loop, walk past the Daybreak Boat Dock until the path meets S. Kestrel Rise Road.

GO FARTHER

Visit the aptly named Sunrise Mountain Park for a stunning panorama of the Wasatch Mountains and an additional 1.5 miles of walking. The path to the park and the park loop itself are completely paved, with some steep sections. Park hours are 5:00 AM to 10:00 PM.

From the section of gravel at the main hike's 3-mile mark, turn left and move through a colorfully painted underpass. Then go left to cross a bridge. Sunset Park is on the left after 0.2 mile. Cross Topview Road and enter Sunrise Mountain Park, keeping left at the next fork. The most comprehensive view of the Wasatch is on the right after a few hundred feet.

Continue straight to walk the Founders Park Loop. Keep right at the next junction after the trail merges with another path. There is an up-close view of the Oquirrh Mountain Utah Temple before the track turns south to complete the loop. Follow your in-route back to rejoin Oquirrh Lake Loop Trail.

42 Blackridge

DISTANCE:	3.5-mile loop
ELEVATION GAIN:	440 feet
HIGH POINT:	5670 feet
DIFFICULTY:	Moderate
TIME:	2 hours
FITNESS:	Walkers, hikers, runners
FAMILY-FRIENDLY:	Yes, and the paved path around Blackridge Reservoir (see Go Farther) is stroller- and ADA-accessible.
DOG-FRIENDLY:	Yes, on-leash. Poop bags and waste bins at the trailhead.
AMENITIES:	Parking, restrooms, picnic tables, playground, swimming, trail signs
CONTACT/MAP:	Herriman City Parks and Recreation
GPS:	40.48000˚N, 112.02215˚W
BEFORE YOU GO:	Blackridge Reservoir hours are 7:30 AM to 9:00 PM, March 15 to November 14, and 7:30 AM to 6:00 PM, November 15 to March 14. Prime wildflower season is spring and early summer. Popular area with mountain bikers. For winter travel, avalanche education and equipment are recommended.

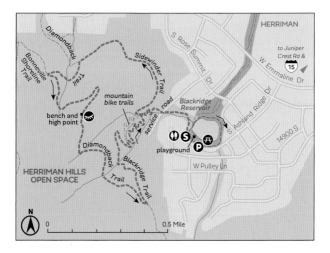

GETTING THERE

Public Transit: Take TRAX Red Line to Daybreak Parkway Station. Request a UTA On Demand ride from the TRAX station to Blackridge Reservoir. **Bike Route:** Use the Salt Lake City & County Bikeways Map to plot a route to the trailhead. **Driving:** From I-15, take exit 289 for UT 154 / Bangerter Highway and travel west for 5 miles. Turn left on 13400 S. drive 1.2 miles, and then turn left on S. Mountain View. After 1 mile, go right on S. Palisade Rose Drive for 0.5 mile, and continue straight for another 0.5 mile when it becomes Juniper Crest Road. Turn right on Emmeline Drive. After 0.2 mile, go left on S. Ashland Ridge Drive; the road ends at the Blackridge Reservoir parking area.

Get a fresh perspective with this 3.5-mile loop—astounding Wasatch views showcase the mountains in a unique light. Foothills burst with native grasses, flowers, and shrubs in spring. You'll begin at Herriman City's Blackridge Reservoir and follow a loop connecting the Blackridge, Sidewinder, and Diamondback Trails.

Herriman, nestled in the foothills of the Oquirrh Mountains, is in the southwest corner of Salt Lake County. Over the past twenty-plus years, the city's population has increased from around 1500 residents to nearly 60,000. One response to Herriman's booming population is its expanding trail network. The recreation paths are expertly designed and make for pleasant walking, but do keep in mind that this area is also popular with mountain bikers.

Avoid this hike on hot days, as there is no shade. Poles and micro-traction spikes are helpful during snowy or icy conditions. Ignore informal side trails and game tracks; follow the obvious, well-worn trail.

GET MOVING

To begin, locate the large trail map and sign at the park's west end. Gently ascend on a well-worn dirt path, surrounded by big sage, bitterbrush, and rabbitbrush. At 0.2 mile, encounter a four-way intersection with a gravel service road; continue straight.

After gaining 75 feet of elevation, encounter a signed T intersection at 0.4 mile. Turn right on Sidewinder and traverse foothills brightly freckled by longleaf phlox, paintbrush, and baby aster in the summer. When the trail turns south, it opens to a thought-provoking view of the Kennecott Copper Mine.

Continue on Sidewinder until it forks at 1 mile (elevation 5390 feet). At the trail sign, go left on the Diamondback to begin a gentle ascent. At 1.2 miles, the trail forks again with the Bonneville Shoreline Trail; go left to stay on Diamondback. Gradually climb, traversing a small ridge. Around 1.7 miles, gain the hike's high point (elevation 5670 feet) and look for a bench with stellar views of the Wasatch Range, including Lone Peak, Mount Timpanogos to the south, and the Broads Fork Twin Peaks across the valley.

Look for a small stand of Rocky Mountain junipers around 2 miles. Follow the trail as it continues to mildly descend and

Big sage and paintbrush fill the slopes along Blackridge.

reach a signed junction with Blackridge at 2.4 miles. Turn left on Blackridge and gradually lose elevation. At 2.9 miles, arrive at a well-signed intersection. To avoid the two down-hill, mountain-bike-only trails, make a hard right, almost a U-turn, to stay on Blackridge. The route zigzags through several switchbacks.

Reach a familiar junction where the trail intercepts Sidewinder, go right, and reverse the route back to the trailhead to complete your 3.5-mile journey.

GO FARTHER

The paved, 0.5-mile loop around Blackridge Reservoir makes a lovely cool down, and the scattered benches offer bird- and people-watching opportunities. To start the loop from the Blackridge trailhead, locate the paved pedestrian path heading toward the reservoir. Follow the walkway as it hugs the reservoir and eventually leads to the sidewalk on the parking lot's perimeter.

GUIDE TO WILDFLOWERS

LEARNING THE NAMES AND SHAPES of indigenous flowers and shrubs makes every nature outing more enjoyable. Using a plant identification app in the field and cross-referencing that information with regional plant guidebooks is immensely rewarding. Over time, the species of wildflowers begin to feel like familiar friends. It becomes a delight to watch the flora change over the seasons and anticipate the rainbow of colors that burst forth with spring blossoms and autumn hues. Use this identification guide to begin an intimate relationship with Salt Lake's plant life.

Opposite: *Paintbrush, fleabane, and wild sticky geranium line the trail through Albion Basin.*

1. Aspen fleabane
2. Arrowleaf balsamroot
3. Big sagebrush
4. Chokecherry
5. Cone flower
6. Fringed bluebell
7. Garrett's fleabane
8. Heartleaf arnica
9. Jacob's-ladder
10. Longleaf phlox
11. Nettleleaf horsemint
12. Oregon grape

13. Pacific ninebark
14. Paintbrush (splitleaf and Wyoming)
15. Richardson's geranium
16. Rocky Mountain blue columbine
17. Rubber rabbitbrush
18. Sego lily
19. Showy goldeneye
20. Showy milkweed
21. Silky lupine
22. Wasatch beardtongue
23. Whorled buckwheat
24. Woods' rose

White Pine Lake (Hike 34) is framed by spires rising out of Little Cottonwood Canyon.

ACKNOWLEDGMENTS

RESEARCHING AND WRITING *Urban Trails: Salt Lake City* was challenging, rewarding, and intimidating. I couldn't have done it without the support and inspiration of my family and friends. First and foremost, thank you to my late granny, Betty Heil, who believed in me from the start, kept me on track throughout the writing process, and accompanied me in her wheelchair on many outings. Other family members were equally important. My late grandma, Doreen Phillips, gifted me a love of stories and language. My husband, Chris Brown, convinced me that I could write a guidebook and supported the effort every step of the way. My father, Stanley Heil, taught me that work is about finding something you love. My mom, Loreen Heil, cheered me on with unwavering confidence and expressed it often. And my brother, Michael Heil, walked and brainstormed with me throughout the entire journey. Thank you all for your love, advice, and steadfast support.

There are countless family members and friends (you know who you are) who showed up to walk and hike with me. Thank you for taking an interest in my project, listening to my ramblings, waiting for wildflowers pictures, and staying constant even at crunch time.

A big thank you to the folks at Mountaineers Books, who provided the opportunity to contribute to the Urban Trails series. I appreciate the clear direction from Kate Rogers, and Janet Kimball throughout the writing process and from my copyeditor, Emily Estes, whose keen eye, word wizardry, and attention to detail improved the book. And thank you, Susan Elderkin, my project editor, who made the final steps fun.

Finally, I give thanks to God for weaving together the complex and majestic tapestry of life, and to great Mother Earth for nurturing my heart, soul, mind, and body.

RESOURCES

CONTACTS AND MAPS

Bonneville Shoreline Trail
bonnevilleshorelinetrail@gmail.com
www.bonnevilleshorelinetrail.org

Cottonwood Heights Parks and Recreation
801-943-31390
https://cottonwoodheights.com/parks

Daybreak Parks and Recreation
801-858-3851
www.daybreakliving.com/parks-recreation.php

Draper Parks and Recreation
Trails and Open Space: 801-576-6571
www.draperutah.gov/1747/Parks-Recreation

Herriman City Parks and Recreation
801-446-5323
www.herriman.org/parks-and-recreation

Jordan River Commission
801-536-4158
https://jordanrivercommission.com

Murray City Parks and Recreation
801-264-2614
www.murray.utah.gov/223/Parks-Recreation

Parley's Rails, Trails and Tunnels (PRATT) Coalition
801-694-8925
www.parleystrail.org

Salt Lake City Public Lands Department
Parks Division: 801-972-7800
Public Lands Administration: 801-972-7800
Trails and Natural Lands Division: 801-972-7800
Urban Forestry Division: 801-972-7818
www.slc.gov/parks

Salt Lake County Sheriff's Search and Rescue Team
801-840-4000
http://saltlakesearchandrescue.org

Salt Lake Public Utilities
801-483-6900
www.slc.gov/utilities

Salt Lake County Parks and Open Space
385-468-7275
https://slco.org/parks
https://slco.org/open-space

Sandy City Parks and Recreation
801-586-7100
https://sandy.utah.gov/407/Parks-and-Recreation

Sugar House Community Council
www.sugarhousecouncil.org/1264-2

Taylorsville Parks and Recreation
801-963-5400
www.taylorsvilleut.gov/our-city/parks-and-recreation

This Is The Place Heritage Park
801-582-1847
www.thisistheplace.org

Town of Alta
801-742-3522
www.alta.com/summer/trail-map

US Forest Service: Uinta-Wasatch-Cache National Forest
801-733-2660
www.fs.usda.gov/uwcnf

University of Utah/Red Butte Garden
801-585-0556
https://redbuttegarden.org

West Jordan Parks Department
801-569-5704
www.westjordan.utah.gov/parks-department

Wheeler Historic Farm
Activity Barn: 385-468-1755
slco.org/wheeler-farm

TRAILS SUPPORT, EDUCATION, COMMUNITY RECREATION, AND CONSERVATION ORGANIZATIONS

Breathe Utah
breathe@breatheutah.org
www.breatheutah.org

Cottonwood Canyons Foundation
801-703-7574
https://cottonwoodcanyons.org

Envision Utah
801-303-1450
https://envisionutah.org

Friends of Alta
801-742-9719
www.friendsofalta.org

Friends of Great Salt Lake
801-583-5593
www.fogsl.org

Great Salt Lake Audubon Society
385-313-0608
https://greatsaltlakeaudubon.org

Hawk Watch International
801-484-6808
https://hawkwatch.org

Heal Utah
801-355-5055
www.healutah.org

National Parks Conservation Association
800-628-7275
www.npca.org

Nature and Human Health Utah
https://natureandhealthutah.org

Peace Gardens International Academy
801-938-5326
www.internationalpeacegardens.org

Salt Lake Climbers Alliance
www.saltlakeclimbers.org

Salt Lake County Watershed Planning and Restoration
385-468-4575
https://slco.org/watershed/about-us

Save Our Canyons
801-363-7283
https://saveourcanyons.org

Seven Canyons Trust
info@sevencanyonstrust.org
https://sevencanyonstrust.org

The Jordan River Foundation
thejordanriverfoundation@gmail.com
https://jrf-utah.org

The Nature Conservancy of Utah
801-531-0999
www.nature.org/en-us/about-us/where-we-work/united-states/utah

Tracy Aviary
801-596-8500
https://tracyaviary.org

Trails Utah
919-220-6292
www.trailsutah.org

Trust for Public Land
303-837-1414
www.tpl.org

Utah Avalanche Center
888-999-4019
https://utahavalanchecenter.org

Utah Department of Environmental Quality
801-536-4123
https://deq.utah.gov

Utah Diné Bikéyah
385-202-4954
https://utahdinebikeyah.org

Utah Division of Wildlife Resources
801-538-4700
https://wildlife.utah.gov

Utah Native Plant Society
www.unps.org/index.html

Utah Open Lands
801-463-6156
www.utahopenlands.org

Utah Reclamation Mitigation and Conservation Commission
801-524-3146
www.mitigationcommission.gov

Utah Rivers Council
801-486-4776
https://utahrivers.org

Wasatch Mountain Club
801-463-9842
www.wasatchmountainclub.org

TRANSPORTATION
Salt Lake City and County Bikeways Map
www.slc.gov/transportation/bike/bikemap

Utah Department of Transportation (UDOT)
801-956-4000
www.udot.utah.gov/connect

Utah Transit Authority (UTA)
801-743-3882
www.rideuta.com

INDEX

ABOUT THE AUTHOR

Ashley Lauren Brown is a Utah native hailing from Pleasant Grove. She spent her childhood playing in the foothills of Mount Timpanogos. Access to the wilderness from a young age molded her life around natural exploration.

A sabbatical after graduation from the University of Utah led her to live in Hawaii, followed by Washington State. The Wasatch Mountains and mystical red deserts of southern Utah brought her home after a few short years.

A love of wilderness and the call to stewardship influence her writing and recreating. It is in the quiet of wild places where she finds wholeness, and she relies on time rambling in the mountains for rejuvenation. With her husband, Chris, an AMGA-certified mountain guide, she finds vision and drive while climbing cliffs and alpine routes or splitboarding the iconic Wasatch Mountains.

Ashley lives with her husband in Salt Lake City, where she contributes to Park City– and Utah-based publications. You can check out her goings-on at www.pennedbynature.com.

recreation • lifestyle • conservation

MOUNTAINEERS BOOKS, including its two imprints, Skipstone and Braided River, is a leading publisher of quality outdoor recreation, sustainability, and conservation titles. As a 501(c)(3) nonprofit, we are committed to supporting the environmental and educational goals of our organization by providing expert information on human-powered adventure, sustainable practices at home and on the trail, and preservation of wilderness.

Our publications are made possible through the generosity of donors, and through sales of 700 titles on outdoor recreation, sustainable lifestyle, and conservation. To donate, purchase books, or learn more, visit us online:

MOUNTAINEERS BOOKS

1001 SW Klickitat Way, Suite 201 • Seattle, WA 98134

800-553-4453 • mbooks@mountaineersbooks.org

www.mountaineersbooks.org

An independent nonprofit publisher since 1960

YOU MAY ALSO LIKE: